Mediterranean Diet Meal Prep

Delicious and Healthy Mediterranean Diet Recipes. Lose Weight, Save Time and Feel Your Best with The Mediterranean Diet

Table of Contents

Introduction

Starting the Mediterranean Diet? Then you've come to the right place! As you may know, getting to know the ins and outs of a new diet can be a real challenge. On top of that, being too busy to cook, not being prepared and eating what you want when hunger strikes can completely set you back. That's where meal prepping comes in!

Meal prepping beforehand will help cut down on cooking time, save you money and make sure you stick to the Mediterranean diet. In my cookbook, I'll be covering how meal prepping your Mediterranean Diet recipes will simply change your whole lifestyle. I'll also be sharing what food you can put on your grocery list, what to avoid, and how to make an amazing meal plan with little effort. Of course, this cookbook wouldn't be complete without recipes, and I have plenty for you to cook!

Now, let's start by jumping into what the Mediterranean Diet is all about and then get into how you can Meal Prep like a pro!

The Mediterranean Diet – Less of a Diet, More of a Lifestyle

When you hear the word *Diet,* you probably think about counting calories and tons of food restrictions.. Thankfully, the Mediterranean Diet is different! It has fewer restrictions, and puts a huge emphasis on enjoying good company, fresh foods, and a glass of red wine if you'd like. Sounds good, right?!

It's also far from being flavorless and boring! The Mediterranean Diet is filled with heart-healthy foods based on delicious and traditional Mediterranean-style recipes. Meaning it features all the basics of healthy eating – including a splash of flavorful olive oil and a daily glass of red wine – along with the traditional cooking style of countries near the Mediterranean Sea.

When you lay it all out the Mediterranean diet consists of:

- Eating primarily plant-based foods, such as vegetables, fruits, whole grains, legumes, and nuts.
- Avoiding unhealthy butter and replacing it with healthy fats such as olive and canola oil
- Using more spices and herbs instead of salt to flavor foods
- Eating poultry and fish at least twice a week
- Limiting your intake of red meats to no more than a few times a month
- Enjoying your meals with family and friends
- Drinking red wine in moderation (optional)
- Getting plenty of exercise and water

The Mediterranean diet also happens to be one of the most researched diets out there. Health experts have thoroughly examined this diet and concluded that it offers plenty of benefits for long-term health, which I'll get into next!

Benefits of Choosing the Mediterranean Diet

Any doctor would tell you that having large quantities of fresh fruits and vegetables, nuts, fish and olive oil— along with heart-pumping physical activity— will make you healthier. And this is exactly what the Mediterranean diet naturally promotes! Here are some of the benefits you can enjoy by following a traditional Mediterranean diet;

Lowers your risk of heart disease and stroke
By following the Mediterranean diet correctly, it will limit your intake of processed foods, refined breads, and red meats, and promotes drinking red wine instead of very hard liquor - these restrictions will help prevent stroke and heart disease.

Keeps you feeling younger
If you happen to be an older adult, the nutrients from the Mediterranean diet can reduce the risk of developing muscle weakness and other signs of frailty by around 70 percent.

Reduces the risk of Alzheimer's disease
Research into the Mediterranean diet has suggested that it may improve blood sugar levels, cholesterol, and overall blood vessel health. In turn, these improvements may reduce your risk of Alzheimer's disease or dementia.

Help with depression and anxiety
People with depression, anxiety, or other mental health issues are often told to make sure their diet is rich in vegetables and healthy fats. Why? This is mainly due to the carotenoids in spinach, kale, and eggs which has been shown to boost the good bacteria in your gut, which in turn will boost your mood. One study also found that when older adults followed the Mediterranean diet, they're less likely to experience symptoms of depression.

Cuts the risk of Parkinson's disease in half
The Mediterranean diet has high levels of antioxidants that can prevent cells from undergoing oxidative stress - a damaging process, which will cut the risk of Parkinson's disease in half.

Protects against cancers
The Mediterranean diet may also help fight off cancer. A systematic review of studies has found that overall, individuals who follow the diet the most have a 13 percent lower rate of a cancerous death compared to those who adhere the least 15 Specific cancers protected against including colorectal cancer, breast cancer, prostate cancer, and head and neck cancer.

Increases longevity
With the Mediterranean Diet you can reduce your risk of developing cancer or heart disease, in turn also reduce your risk of death at any age by 20%.

Protects against type 2 diabetes
This diet happens to be rich in fiber which is digests slowly and prevents huge highs/lows dips in your blood sugar.

Promotes healthy weight management
As I mentioned before, the Mediterranean diet is rich in fiber so it will help you stay fuller longer and helps with healthy weight and metabolism. This is all due to replacing simple carbohydrates with fibrous fruits, legumes, vegetables, and beans.

Really good for your gut
Another study found that people who are on the Mediterranean diet had higher levels of good bacteria in their microbiome, compared to people who were following a traditional Western diet. The researchers also noted that eating plant-based foods like vegetables, fruits, and legumes had increased the good bacteria by 7 percent.

The Mediterranean Diet – What You Can and Can't Eat

Although the Mediterranean diet isn't too restrictive, there are foods you have to incorporate more of into your diet and foods you have to skip. I'll get into everything you need to know about what you can eat and what you should avoid in detail below.

Foods to Shop For

Vegetables and Fruits – You can enjoy all fruits and vegetables out there on the Mediterranean diet! Some of the most popular veggie choices on this diet include spinach, tomatoes, broccoli, kale, cauliflower, carrots, artichokes, and eggplant. As for fruits, popular choices include apples, oranges, bananas, strawberries, grapes, etc.

Fish and Seafood – Here's your main source of protein – you can eat fresh seafood and fish at least twice a week, or more. Popular choices include haddock, tuna, salmon, shrimp along with shellfish like lobster, mussels, crab, oysters.

Nuts and Seeds – Love the crunch! Nuts and seeds will be your second sources of protein, healthy fats, and contain unsaturated fatty acids and omega-3 fatty acids. So, make sure to add almonds, hazelnuts, cashews, sunflower seeds, walnuts, and pumpkin seeds to your shopping list - always unsalted and non-candied.
And please note that even though nuts and seeds have healthy fats they are still high in calories, so stick to just having an ounce or two per day.

Legumes – You can make meals with beans, lentils, peanuts, peas, chickpeas, etc.

Whole Grains, Whole-Grain Breads, Potatoes – This includes white potatoes, turnips, sweet potatoes, whole wheat bread, whole wheat pasta, whole oats, brown rice, rye, barley, couscous, and buckwheat.
Only whole grain breads and pastas are recommended, so avoid processed white breads and pasta.

Herbs & Spices – Pepper, basil, cinnamon, parsley, rosemary, thyme, mint, etc.

Healthy Fats – Remember! The Mediterranean diet promotes eating **healthy fats and oils with unsaturated fatty acids** and not saturated fats - which are really bad for your body. Extra virgin olive oil is one awesome healthy fat, you can also incorporate other healthy fats such as avocado oil, coconut oil, olives, avocados, and more.

Important! What you can do about the Mercury Found in Fish
The Mediterranean Diet calls for tons of tasty fish and seafood dishes! But even though they have plenty of health benefits, nearly all fish and shellfish today contain traces of pollutants, including toxic metal mercury. Follow these guidelines below to help you make the safest choices for you and your family.

- It's safe for most adults to eat about 12 oz. (or two 6-ounce servings) of other kinds of cooked seafood a week.
- Larger fish have a higher concentration of mercury and other pollutants, so it's best to avoid eating large fish like swordfish, shark, tilefish, and king mackerel.
- Women who are pregnant, nursing mothers, and children aged 12 and younger should eat fish and shellfish that are lower in mercury, including shrimp, canned light tuna, Pollock, salmon or catfish. Because albacore tuna is higher in mercury content, you should eat no more than 6 oz (one average meal) per week. If you're doing your own fishing, learn more about the fish you've caught from local seafood experts to know if it's safe to eat.

Foods You Can Enjoy from Time to Time in Moderation

Moderation is key when it comes to the Mediterranean Diet. Below are foods you can eat BUT ONLY every now and then.

- **Red Meat.** Red meat (steak, ground beef, etc.) is rarely included on the Mediterranean diet. If you would like to have red meat, it should only be consumed very infrequently. In fact, red meats are limited – just 12-16 oz. per month. So, save it for a juicy steak!
- **Poultry**. Chicken, turkey, duck, quail etc.
- **Dairy.** Low fat and fat-free dairy such as low-fat milk, yogurt, cheese can be consumed. Have these lower-fat options instead of full-fat dairy.
- **Eggs.** All types of eggs are encouraged in moderation since they are a protein source and can be cooked in many ways.

Unhealthy Foods to Avoid

You'll need to be mindful of avoiding these kinds of food in the future!
- **Highly Processed Foods.** It's a well-known fact that processed foods are bad for you! That's one of the reasons why they're not allowed on the Mediterranean diet. Basically, the golden rule to follow is if it comes in a box, don't eat it! This rule also goes for foods that are marketed as "diet" or "low fat," since these are still highly processed.
- **Refined Grains.** Whole grains are allowed in the Mediterranean diet, but all refined grains are excluded. This includes white bread, refined pasta (aka the normal kind), refined bagels, cereal, etc.
- **Added Sugars.** Avoid added sugars of all kinds this includes ice cream, candy, chocolate, sugary sodas, etc.

- **Trans or Saturated Fats.** Butter, margarine, etc.
- **Processed Meats.** Avoid heavily processed meats like sausages, hot dogs, and bacon
- **Refined Oils.** Oils like soybean oil, vegetable oil, and cottonseed oil are not to be used. Stick with olive oil and healthy oils instead!

What to Drink

If you love wine good news! The Mediterranean diet does allow you to drink red wine. Those on the diet can have 1 glass of wine per day if you'd like.
Of course, good old water needs to be consumed heavily! Tea and coffee are allowed. But sugary sodas and fruits need to be avoided.

Get Started on The Mediterranean Diet

The beauty of the Mediterranean diet is how simple it is. That's why it's important to not overthink it when you're changing your current meal plan to the Mediterranean diet! Below, I'll show you how you can start changing your eating habits and give you a glimpse of what your 1st week on the Mediterranean diet will look like with a sample menu.

How to Transition into the Mediterranean Diet

Yes, changing your eating habits for the better can be an amazing, yet daunting task. Here are a few suggestions for you:

Eat lots of vegetables.

Soups, salad, and crudités platters are a great way to eat more veggies.

Don't Skip breakfast.

Start your day with whole grains, fruits, and other fiber-rich foods to keep you full for hours.

Make sure you plan to eat seafood twice a week.

Fish such as salmon, tuna, herring, sardines, and sablefish are rich in Omega-3 fatty acids. Shellfish like mussels, oysters, and clams have similar benefits for brain and heart health.

Create a vegetarian meal once a week.

It's helpful to jump on the "Meatless Mondays" trend and avoid meat on the first day of the week or pick a day to build your meals around vegetables, beans, and whole grains. Once you get the hang of it, try two nights a week.

Enjoy dairy products in moderation.

If you didn't know, the USDA recommends limiting saturated fats to no more than 10% of your daily calories (that's about 200 calories for most people). You're still allowed to enjoy dairy products such as natural cheese (unprocessed), plain or Greek yogurt.

For dessert, opt for fresh fruit.

Instead of reaching for ice cream, cake or other kinds of baked goods, opt for healthy fruits such as grapes, strawberries, fresh figs, or apples.

Use ONLY the good fats.

You can enjoy healthy fats in your daily meals by using extra-virgin olive oil, nuts, sunflower seeds, olives, and avocados.

Meal Prepping 101

If this is your first-time meal prepping, the idea of creating a menu, and cooking the food a few days in advance can overwhelm you. But don't worry! It's easy to get everything finished just like a meal prep pro when you follow my 4 steps and tips below.

Step 1. Schedule in the Time to Prep

It can take a few hours or a whole afternoon to prep for a few days. So, make sure you pencil in a few hours into your schedule for prepping day.

Step 2. Buy the RIGHT Containers

Get ready for Prep Day by having all the right containers where you can see them! By right, I mean containers that are all the same size and can easily divide up food with compartments.

Make sure that all of these prep containers are made of BPA- Free plastic or glass. Also, have plenty of Mason jars with lids on hand for salads and dressings.

Step 3. Create a Plan

Of course, you need to know what you're going to cook before prep day. So, make sure you pick out the recipes you want to try for that week and create a menu to make everything easier.

Step 4. Write Down Your Grocery List

Now, that you have all your recipes for the week ready, it's time to hit the grocery store. Just make sure you Only buy what's on the list and nothing more!

And you're all done and ready for prep day!

Meal Prepping Tips You Need to Know

Ensure that prep day is a breeze with these ESSENTIAL tips!

Don't go overboard

Don't ever try to meal prep breakfast, lunch and dinner for the entire week. I'm warning you, if you make this mistake, you'll definitely go crazy. Instead, figure out when you're super busy and create a meal plan around that.

For example, if you don't have time for lunch or want to stay out of the kitchen for dinner, ONLY make lunch or dinner for the week.

Keep Your Food Fresh and Label Everything

Always label and write the expiration dates on your containers. Also, if you're selecting recipes that aren't in my cookbook make sure they're ones that won't taste weird after being in the fridge for a few days.

Prepare to Eat Your Meals within 3-4 days

Not all dishes you meal prep will last in your fridge for an entire week, so double check and see if you can freeze anything you can't eat within 3-4 days.

Let Your Food Cool Down

Allow all your food to cool down completely before storing it in the freezer. If you don't, you'll change the texture of the food and make it taste terrible. You'll also partially thaw the food in the freezer when you place a hot meal in there and cause them to refreeze later – which will change their taste and texture too.

Allow the food to properly cool after cooking by placing it in a wide, shallow container and refrigerate, uncovered, until cooled. If you've cooked a soup, stew or chili, cool them in an ice bath by placing them into a metal bowl in another bowl with ice and water.

Introduction to Recipes

Now that you know all about the Mediterranean Diet and how to meal prep like a pro, it's time to explore the rest of my cookbook and come up with your own meal plan! I'll be providing you with plenty of interesting choices that are far from boring and easy to create. Just pick and choose what you'd like to enjoy during the week, and you're done!

Breakfast

Mediterranean Scrambled Eggs

You'll love these amazing Mediterranean scrambled eggs made with yellow peppers, cherry tomatoes, spring onions, olives, herbs and capers in the morning!

Prep Time: 5 minutes
Cook Time: 10 minutes
Total Time: 15 minutes
Servings: 2

Ingredients:

- 1 tbsp oil
- 1 yellow pepper, diced
- 2 spring onions, sliced
- 8 cherry tomatoes, quartered
- 2 tbsp sliced black olives
- 1 tbsp capers
- 4 eggs
- 1/4 tsp dried oregano
- Black pepper

Topping:

- Fresh parsley, to serve

Directions:

1. In a frying pan over medium heat, add the oil
2. Once heated, add the diced pepper and chopped spring onions, cook for a few minutes, until slightly soft
3. Add in the quartered tomatoes, olives and capers, and cook for 1 more minute
4. Crack the eggs into the pan, immediately scramble with a spoon or spatula
5. Sprinkle with oregano and plenty of black pepper, and stir until the eggs are fully cooked
6. Distribute the eggs evenly into the containers, store in the fridge for 2-3 days

To Serve: Reheat in the microwave for 30 seconds or in a toaster oven until warmed through

Nutritional Facts Per Serving: Calories:249 | Carbs: 13g| Total Fat: 17g | Protein: 14g

Greek Yogurt with Fresh Berries, Honey and Nuts

Dig into a delicious bowl of Greek yogurt topped with fresh berries, honey and nuts!

Prep Time: 5 minutes

Total Time: 5 minutes

Servings: 1

Ingredient:

- 6 oz. nonfat plain Greek yogurt
- 1/2 cup fresh berries of your choice
- 1 tbsp .25 oz crushed walnuts
- 1 tbsp honey

Directions:

1. In a jar with a lid, add the yogurt
2. Top with berries and a drizzle of honey
3. Top with the lid and store in the fridge for 2-3 days

To Serve: Add the granola or nuts, enjoy

Nutritional Facts Per Serving: Calories:250 | Carbs: 35g| Total Fat: 4g | Protein: 19g

Mediterranean Egg Muffins with Ham

With a tasty Mediterranean flair, these savory breakfast muffins are made with ham, peppers, spinach, and feta cheese!

Prep Time: 10 minutes
Cook Time: 15 minutes
Total Time: 25 minutes
Yields: 6 muffins

Ingredients:

- 9 Slices of thin cut deli ham
- 1/2 cup canned roasted red pepper, sliced + additional for garnish
- 1/3 cup fresh spinach, minced
- 1/4 cup feta cheese, crumbled
- 5 large eggs
- Pinch of salt
- Pinch of pepper
- 1 1/2 tbsp Pesto sauce
- Fresh basil for garnish

Directions:

1. Preheat oven to 400 degrees F
2. Spray a muffin tin with cooking spray, generously
3. Line each of the muffin tin with 1 ½ pieces of ham - making sure there aren't any holes for the egg mixture come out of
4. Place some of the roasted red pepper in the bottom of each muffin tin
5. Place 1 tbsp of minced spinach on top of each red pepper
6. Top the pepper and spinach off with a large 1/2 tbsp of crumbled feta cheese
7. In a medium bowl, whisk together the eggs salt and pepper, divide the egg mixture evenly among the 6 muffin tins
8. Bake for 15 to 17 minutes until the eggs are puffy and set
9. Remove each cup from the muffin tin
10. Allow to cool completely
11. Distribute the muffins among the containers, store in the fridge for 2 - 3days or in the freezer for 3 months

To Serve: Heat in the microwave for 30 seconds or until heated through. Garnish with 1/4 tsp pesto sauce, additional roasted red pepper slices and fresh basil.

Nutritional Facts Per Serving: Calories:109 | Carbs: 2g| Total Fat: 6g | Protein: 9g

Quinoa Bake with Banana

A mixed of sweet bananas, molasses, and spices come together to create this inviting gingerbread quinoa bake.

Prep Time: 10 minutes
Cook Time: 1 hr 20 minutes
Total Time: 1 hr 30 minutes
Servings: 8

Ingredients:

- 3 cups medium over-ripe Bananas, mashed
- 1/4 cup molasses
- 1/4 cup pure maple syrup
- 1 tbsp cinnamon
- 2 tsp raw vanilla extract
- 1 tsp ground ginger
- 1 tsp ground cloves
- 1/2 tsp ground allspice
- 1/2 tsp salt
- 1 cup quinoa, uncooked
- 2 1/2 cups unsweetened vanilla almond milk
- 1/4 cup slivered almonds

Directions:

1. In the bottom of a 2 1/2-3-quart casserole dish, mix together the mashed banana, maple syrup, cinnamon, vanilla extract, ginger, cloves, allspice, molasses, and salt until well mixed
2. Add in the quinoa, stir until the quinoa is evenly in the banana mixture.
3. Whisk in the almond milk, mix until well combined, cover and refrigerate overnight or bake immediately
4. Heat oven to 350 degrees F
5. Whisk the quinoa mixture making sure it doesn't settle to the bottom
6. Cover the pan with tinfoil and bake until the liquid is absorbed, and the top of the quinoa is set, about 1 hour to 1 hour and 15 mins
7. Turn the oven to high broil, uncover the pan, sprinkle with sliced almonds, and lightly press them into the quinoa
8. Broil until the almonds just turn golden brown, about 2-4 minutes, watching closely, as they burn quickly
9. Allow to cool for 10 minutes then slice the quinoa bake
10. Distribute the quinoa bake among the containers, store in the fridge for 3-4 days

Nutritional Facts Per Serving: Calories:213 | Carbs: 41g| Total Fat: 4g | Protein: 5g

Italian Breakfast Sausage with Baby Potatoes and Vegetables

On one baking sheet, you can create a delicious dish made with Italian sausages and plenty of roasted vegetables!

Prep Time: 10 Minutes
Cook Time: 30 Minutes
Total Time: 40 Minutes
Serves: 4

Ingredients:

- 1 lbs sweet Italian sausage links, sliced on the bias (diagonal)
- 2 cups baby potatoes, halved
- 2 cups broccoli florets
- 1 cup onions cut to 1-inch chunks
- 2 cups small mushrooms -half or quarter the large ones for uniform size
- 1 cup baby carrots
- 2 tbsp olive oil
- 1/2 tsp garlic powder
- 1/2 tsp Italian seasoning
- 1 tsp salt
- 1/2 tsp pepper

Directions:

1. Preheat the oven to 400 degrees F
2. In a large bowl, add the baby potatoes, broccoli florets, onions, small mushrooms, and baby carrots
3. Add in the olive oil, salt, pepper, garlic powder and Italian seasoning and toss to evenly coat
4. Spread the vegetables onto a sheet pan in one even layer
5. Arrange the sausage slices on the pan over the vegetables
6. Bake for 30 minutes – make sure to sake halfway through to prevent sticking
7. Allow to cool
8. Distribute the Italian sausages and vegetables among the containers and store in the fridge for 2-3 days

To Serve: Reheat in the microwave for 1-2 minutes, or until heated through and enjoy!

Recipe Notes: If you would like crispier potatoes, place them on the pan and bake for 10-15 minutes before adding the other ingredients to the pan.

Nutrition Facts Per Serving: Calories:321 | Total Fat: 16g| Total Carbs: 23g| Fiber: 4g| Protein: 22g

Sun dried Tomatoes, Dill and Feta Omelette Casserole

Infused with flavor from the sun-dried tomato feta cheese and fresh dill, you can't go wrong with this dish for breakfast!

Prep Time: 10
Cook Time: 40
Total Time: 50
Servings: 6

Ingredients:

- 12 large eggs
- 2 cups whole milk
- 8 oz fresh spinach
- 2 cloves garlic, minced
- 12 oz artichoke salad with olives and peppers, drained and chopped
- 5 oz sun dried tomato feta cheese, crumbled
- 1 tbsp fresh chopped dill or 1 tsp dried dill
- 1 tsp dried oregano
- 1 tsp lemon pepper
- 1 tsp salt
- 4 tsp olive oil, divided

Directions:

1. Preheat oven to 375 degrees F
2. Chop the fresh herbs and artichoke salad
3. In a skillet over medium heat, add 1 tbsp olive oil
4. Sauté the spinach and garlic until wilted, about 3 minutes
5. Oil a 9x13 inch baking dish, layer the spinach and artichoke salad evenly in the dish
6. In a medium bowl, whisk together the eggs, milk, herbs, salt and lemon pepper
7. Pour the egg mixture over vegetables, sprinkle with feta cheese
8. Bake in the center of the oven for 35-40 minutes until firm in the center
9. Allow to cool, slice a and distribute among the storage containers. Store for 2-3 days or freeze for 3 months

To Serve: Reheat in the microwave for 30 seconds or until heated through or in the toaster oven for 5 minutes or until heated through

Nutritional Facts Per Serving: Calories:196 | Total Carbohydrates: 5g| Total Fat: 12g | Protein: 10g

Mediterranean Breakfast Egg White Sandwich

The roasted tomatoes, egg whites, fresh herbs, pesto and cheese on this sandwich makes it great for a quick and flavorful breakfast!

Prep Time: 10 minutes
Cook Time: 30 minutes
Total Time: 40 minutes
Servings 1

Ingredients:

- 1 tsp vegan butter
- ¼ cup egg whites
- 1 tsp chopped fresh herbs such as parsley, basil, rosemary
- 1 whole grain seeded ciabatta roll
- 1 tbsp pesto
- 1-2 slices muenster cheese (or other cheese such as provolone, Monterey Jack, etc.)
- About ½ cup roasted tomatoes
- Salt, to taste
- Pepper, to taste

Roasted Tomatoes:

- 10 oz grape tomatoes
- 1 tbsp extra virgin olive oil
- Kosher salt, to taste
- Coarse black pepper, to taste

Directions:

1. In a small nonstick skillet over medium heat, melt the vegan butter
2. Pour in egg whites, season with salt and pepper, sprinkle with fresh herbs, cook for 3-4 minutes or until egg is done, flip once
3. In the meantime, toast the ciabatta bread in toaster
4. Once done, spread both halves with pesto
5. Place the egg on the bottom half of sandwich roll, folding if necessary, top with cheese, add the roasted tomatoes and top half of roll sandwich
6. To make the roasted tomatoes: Preheat oven to 400 degrees F. Slice tomatoes in half lengthwise. Then place them onto a baking sheet and drizzle with the olive oil, toss to coat. Season with salt and pepper and roast in oven for about 20 minutes, until the skin appears wrinkled

Nutritional Facts Per Serving: Calories:458 | Total Carbohydrates: 51g| Total Fat: 0g | Protein: 21g

Breakfast Taco Scramble

Jazz up your morning with this Breakfast Taco Scramble recipe! It calls for potatoes, scramble eggs, turkey taco meat and salsa.

Prep Time: 10 Minutes
Cook Time: 1 Hour 25 Minutes
Total Time: 1 Hour 35 Minutes
Serves: 4

Ingredients:

- 8 large eggs, beaten
- 1/4 tsp seasoning salt
- 1 lb 99% lean ground turkey
- 2 tbsp Greek seasoning
- 1/2 small onion, minced
- 2 tbsp bell pepper, minced
- 4 oz. can tomato sauce
- 1/4 cup water
- 1/4 cup chopped scallions or cilantro, for topping

For the potatoes:

- 12 (1 lb) baby gold or red potatoes, quartered
- 4 tsp olive oil
- 3/4 tsp salt
- 1/2 tsp garlic powder
- fresh black pepper, to taste

Directions:

1. In a large bowl, beat the eggs, season with seasoning salt
2. Preheat the oven to 425 degrees F
3. Spray a 9x12 or large oval casserole dish with cooking oil
4. Add the potatoes 1 tbsp oil, 3/4 teaspoon salt, garlic powder and black pepper and toss to coat
5. Bake for 45 minutes to 1 hour, tossing every 15 minutes
6. In the meantime, brown the turkey in a large skillet over medium heat, breaking it up while it cooks
7. Once no longer pink, add in the Greek seasoning
8. Add in the bell pepper, onion, tomato sauce and water, stir and cover, simmer on low for about 20 minutes
9. Spray a different skillet with nonstick spray over medium heat

10. Once heated, add in the eggs seasoned with 1/4 tsp of salt and scramble for 2–3 minutes, or cook until it sets
11. Distribute 3/4 cup turkey and 2/3 cup eggs and divide the potatoes in each storage container, store for 3-4 days

To Serve: Reheat in the microwave for 1-minute (until 90% heated through) top with shredded cheese if desired, and chopped scallions

Nutrition Facts Per Serving (¼ of a the scramble): Calories:450 | Total Fat: 19g| Total Carbs: 24.5g| Fiber: 4g| Protein: 46g

Blueberry Greek Yogurt Pancakes

Make regular breakfast pancakes a little more special by using Greek Yogurt and blueberries!

Prep Time: 15 minutes
Cook Time: 15 minutes
Total Time: 30 minutes
Servings: 6

Ingredients:

- 1 1/4 cup all-purpose flour
- 2 tsp baking powder
- 1 tsp baking soda
- 1/4 tsp salt
- 1/4 cup sugar
- 3 eggs
- 3 tbsp vegan butter unsalted, melted
- 1/2 cup milk
- 1 1/2 cups Greek yogurt plain, non-fat
- 1/2 cup blueberries optional

Toppings:

- Greek yogurt
- Mixed berries – blueberries, raspberries and blackberries

Directions:

1. In a large bowl, whisk together the flour, salt, baking powder and baking soda
2. In a separate bowl, whisk together butter, sugar, eggs, Greek yogurt, and milk until the mixture is smooth
3. Then add in the Greek yogurt mixture from step to the dry mixture in step 1, mix to combine, allow the patter to sit for 20 minutes to get a smooth texture – if using blueberries fold them into the pancake batter
4. Heat the pancake griddle, spray with non-stick butter spray or just brush with butter
5. Pour the batter, in 1/4 cupful's, onto the griddle
6. Cook until the bubbles on top burst and create small holes, lift up the corners of the pancake to see if they're golden browned on the bottom
7. With a wide spatula, flip the pancake and cook on the other side until lightly browned
8. Distribute the pancakes in among the storage containers, store in the fridge for 3 day or in the freezer for 2 months

To Serve: Reheat microwave for 1 minute (until 80% heated through) or on the stove top, drizzle warm syrup on top, scoop of Greek yogurt, and mixed berries (including blueberries, raspberries, blackberries)

Nutritional Facts Per Serving: Calories:258 | Total Carbohydrates: 33g| Total Fat: 8g | Protein: 11g

Cauliflower Fritters with Hummus

Start your day off right with delicious cauliflower fitters and creamy hummus!

Prep Time: 15 minutes

Cook Time: 15 minutes

Total Time: 30 minutes

Servings: 4

Ingredients:

- 2 (15 oz) cans chickpeas, divided
- 2 1/2 tbsp olive oil, divided, plus more for frying
- 1 cup onion, chopped, about 1/2 a small onion
- 2 tbsp garlic, minced
- 2 cups cauliflower, cut into small pieces, about 1/2 a large head
- 1/2 tsp salt
- black pepper

Topping:

- Hummus, of choice
- Green onion, diced

Directions:

1. Preheat oven to 400°F
2. Rinse and drain 1 can of the chickpeas, place them on a paper towel to dry off well
3. Then place the chickpeas into a large bowl, removing the loose skins that come off, and toss with 1 tbsp of olive oil, spread the chickpeas onto a large pan (being careful not to over-crowd them) and sprinkle with salt and pepper
4. Bake for 20 minutes, then stir, and then bake an additional 5-10 minutes until very crispy
5. Once the chickpeas are roasted, transfer them to a large food processor and process until broken down and crumble - Don't over process them and turn it into flour, as you need to have some texture. Place the mixture into a small bowl, set aside
6. In a large pan over medium-high heat, add the remaining 1 1/2 tbsp of olive oil
7. Once heated, add in the onion and garlic, cook until lightly golden brown, about 2 minutes. Then add in the chopped cauliflower, cook for an additional 2 minutes, until the cauliflower is golden
8. Turn the heat down to low and cover the pan, cook until the cauliflower is fork tender and the onions are golden brown and caramelized, stirring often, about 3-5 minutes
9. Transfer the cauliflower mixture to the food processor, drain and rinse the remaining can of chickpeas and add them into the food processor, along with the

salt and a pinch of pepper. Blend until smooth, and the mixture starts to ball, stop to scrape down the sides as needed

10. Transfer the cauliflower mixture into a large bowl and add in 1/2 cup of the roasted chickpea crumbs (you won't use all of the crumbs, but it is easier to break them down when you have a larger amount.), stir until well combined

11. In a large bowl over medium heat, add in enough oil to lightly cover the bottom of a large pan

12. Working in batches, cook the patties until golden brown, about 2-3 minutes, flip and cook again

13. Distribute among the container, placing parchment paper in between the fritters. Store in the fridge for 2-3 days

To Serve: Heat through in the oven at 350F for 5-8 minutes. Top with hummus, green onion and enjoy!

Recipe Notes: Don't add too much oil while frying the fritter or they will end up soggy. Use only enough to cover the pan. Use a fork while frying and resist the urge to flip them every minute to see if they are golden

Nutritional Facts Per Serving: Calories:333 | Total Carbohydrates: 45g| Total Fat: 13g | Protein: 14g

Overnight Berry Chia Oats

So quick and easy, this recipe for overnight berry chia oats are a healthy breakfast you can grab on your busiest day!

Prep Time: 5 minutes
Cook Time: 5 minutes
Total Time: 10 minutes
Servings: 1

Ingredients:

- 1/2 cup Quaker Oats rolled oats
- 1/4 cup chia seeds
- 1 cup milk or water
- pinch of salt and cinnamon
- maple syrup, or a different sweetener, to taste
- 1 cup frozen berries of choice or smoothie leftovers

Toppings:

- Yogurt
- Berries

Directions:

1. In a jar with a lid, add the oats, seeds, milk, salt, and cinnamon, refrigerate overnight
2. On serving day, puree the berries in a blender
3. Stir the oats, add in the berry puree and top with yogurt and more berries, nuts, honey, or garnish of your choice
4. Enjoy!

Recipe Notes: Make 3 jars at a time in individual jars for easy grab and go breakfasts for the next few days.

Nutritional Facts Per Serving: Calories:405 | Carbs: 65g| Total Fat: 11g | Protein: 17g

Shakshuka With Feta

Bright, tasty and a bit spicy, this one-skillet recipe features a delicious tomato-red pepper sauce with baked eggs and feta cheese.

Prep Time: minutes
Cook Time: minutes
Total Time: minutes
Servings: 4-6

Ingredients:
- 6 large eggs
- 3 tbsp extra-virgin olive oil
- 1 large onion, halved and thinly sliced
- 1 large red bell pepper, seeded and thinly sliced
- 3 garlic cloves, thinly sliced
- 1 tsp ground cumin
- 1 tsp sweet paprika
- ⅛ tsp cayenne, or to taste
- 1 (28-ounce) can whole plum tomatoes with juices, coarsely chopped
- ¾ tsp salt, more as needed
- ¼ tsp black pepper, more as needed
- 5 oz feta cheese, crumbled, about 1 1/4 cups

To Serve:
- Chopped cilantro
- Hot sauce

Directions:
1. Preheat oven to 375 degrees F
2. In a large skillet over medium-low heat, add the oil
3. Once heated, add the onion and bell pepper, cook gently until very soft, about 20 minutes
4. Add in the garlic and cook until tender, 1 to 2 minutes, then stir in cumin, paprika and cayenne, and cook 1 minute
5. Pour in tomatoes, season with 3/4 tsp salt and 1/4 tsp pepper, simmer until tomatoes have thickened, about 10 minutes
6. Then stir in crumbled feta
7. Gently crack eggs into skillet over tomatoes, season with salt and pepper
8. Transfer skillet to oven
9. Bake until eggs have just set, 7 to 10 minutes
10. Allow to cool and distribute among the containers, store in the fridge for 2-3 days

To Serve: Reheat in the oven at 360 degrees F for 5 minutes or until heated through

Nutritional Facts Per Serving: Calories:337 | Carbs: 17g| Total Fat: 25g | Protein: 12g

Mediterranean Stuffed Sweet Potatoes with Chickpeas and Avocado Tahini

Top with an avocado tahini sauce, these Mediterranean stuffed sweet potatoes are filled with zesty marinated chickpeas.

Prep Time: 10 minutes
Cook Time: 40 minutes
Total Time: 50 minutes
Servings: 4

Ingredients:

- 8 medium sized sweet potatoes, rinsed well

Marinated Chickpeas:

- 1 (15 oz) can chickpeas, drained and rinsed
- 1/2 red pepper, diced
- 3 tbsp extra virgin olive oil
- 1 tbsp fresh lemon juice
- 1 tbsp lemon zest
- 1 clove | about 1/2 teaspoon garlic, crushed
- 1 tbsp freshly chopped parsley
- 1 tbsp fresh oregano
- 1/4 tsp sea salt

Avocado Tahini Sauce:

- 1 medium sized ripe avocado
- 1/4 cup tahini
- 1/4 cup water
- 1 clove garlic, crushed
- 1 tbsp fresh parsley
- 1 tbsp fresh lemon juice

Toppings:

- 1/4 cup pepitas, hulled pumpkin seeds
- Crumbled vegan feta or regular feta

Directions:

1. Preheat the oven to 400 degrees F
2. With a fork to pierce a few holes in the sweet potatoes
3. Place them on a baking sheet and bake for 45 minutes to an hour, or until the potatoes are tender to the touch. (Note that larger sweet potato will take longer to bake)
4. In the meantime, prepare the chickpeas by placing them in a medium sized bowl, combine the chickpeas with the extra virgin olive oil, lemon juice, lemon zest, red

bell peppers, garlic, parsley, oregano, and sea salt. Toss the chickpeas until they're all coated in the marinade, set aside

Avocado Tahini Sauce:

1. Create the sauce by adding the ripe avocado, tahini, water, garlic, parsley, and lemon juice into a blender and process until smooth - If you would like a thinned consistency add another 1-2 tbsp of water
2. Once smooth transfer the sauce to a small bowl, set aside

To Assembly:

1. Once the sweet potatoes are tender, remove them from the oven and set aside until they are cool enough to handle
2. Then cut a slit down the middle of each potato and carefully spoon the chickpeas inside
3. Place the potato and chickpeas bake into container, store for 2-3 days

To Serve: Heat through in the oven at 374 degrees F for 5-8 minutes or until heated through. Top with the avocado tahini and sprinkle the pepitas and crumbled feta. Enjoy

Recipe Notes: There will be leftover chickpeas & avocado tahini - save the extras to make more sweet potatoes or create a big salad for a different lunch

Nutritional Facts Per Serving: Calories:308 | Carbs: 38g| Total Fat: 15g | Protein: 7g

Peanut Butter Banana Greek Yogurt

Creamy vanilla Greek yogurt, banana slices and melted peanut butter to create this easy protein-packed yogurt bowl in minutes!

Prep Time: 5 Minutes

Total Time: 5 Minutes

Serves: 4

Ingredients

- 3 cups vanilla Greek yogurt
- 2 medium bananas sliced
- 1/4 cup creamy natural peanut butter
- 1/4 cup flaxseed meal
- 1 tsp nutmeg

Directions:

1. Divide yogurt between four jars with lids
2. Top with banana slices
3. In a bowl, melt the peanut butter in a microwave safe bowl for 30-40 seconds and drizzle one tbsp on each bowl on top of the bananas
4. Store in the fridge for up to 3 days
5. When ready to serve, sprinkle with flaxseed meal and ground nutmeg
6. Enjoy!

Nutritional Facts Per Serving: Calories:370| Carbs: 47g| Total Fat: 10g | Protein: 22g

Veggie Mediterranean Quiche

Fall in love with the bright flavors of this healthy vegetarian Mediterranean Quiche!

Prep Time: 15 minutes

Cook Time: 55 minutes

Total Time: minutes

Servings: 8

Ingredients:

- 1/2 cup sundried tomatoes - dry or in olive oil*
- Boiling water
- 1 prepared pie crust
- 2 tbsp vegan butter
- 1 onion, diced
- 2 cloves garlic, minced
- 1 red pepper, diced
- 1/4 cup sliced Kalamata olives
- 1 tsp dried oregano
- 1 tsp dried parsley
- 1/3 cup crumbled feta cheese
- 4 large eggs
- 1 1/4 cup milk
- 2 cups fresh spinach or 1/2 cup frozen spinach, thawed and squeezed dry
- Salt, to taste
- Pepper, to taste
- 1 cup shredded cheddar cheese, divided

Directions:

1. If you're using dry sundried tomatoes - In a measure cup, add the sundried tomatoes and pour the boiling water over until just covered, allow to sit for 5 minutes or until the tomatoes are soft. The drain and chop tomatoes, set aside
2. Preheat oven to 375 degrees F
3. Fit a 9-inch pie plate with the prepared pie crust, then flute edges, and set aside
4. In a skillet over medium high heat, melt the butter
5. Add in the onion and garlic, and cook until fragrant and tender, about 3 minutes
6. Add in the red pepper, cook for an additional 3 minutes, or until the peppers are just tender
7. Add in the spinach, olives, oregano, and parsley, cook until the spinach is wilted (if you're using fresh) or heated through (if you're using frozen), about 5 minutes

8. Remove the pan from heat, stir in the feta cheese and tomatoes, spoon the mixture into the prepared pie crust, spreading out evenly, set aside
9. In a medium-sized mixing bowl, whisk together the eggs, 1/2 cup of the cheddar cheese, milk, salt, and pepper
10. Pour this egg and cheese mixture evenly over the spinach mixture in the pie crust
11. Sprinkle top with the remaining cheddar cheese
12. Bake for 50-55 minutes, or until the crust is golden brown and the egg is set
13. Allow to cool completely before slicing
14. Wrap the slices in plastic wrap and then aluminum foil and place in the freezer.

To Serve: Remove the aluminum foil and plastic wrap, and microwave for 2 minutes, then allow to rest for 30 seconds, enjoy!

Recipe Notes: You'll find two types of sundried tomatoes available in your local grocery store—dry ones and ones packed in olive oil. Both will work for this recipe.

If you decide to use dry ones, follow the directions in the recipe to reconstitute them. If you're using oil-packed sundried tomatoes, skip the first step and just remove them from the oil, chop them, and continue with the recipe.

Season carefully! Between the feta, cheddar, and olives, this recipe is naturally salty.

Nutritional Facts Per Serving: Calories:239 | Carbs: 19g| Total Fat: 15g | Protein: 7g

Spinach, Feta and Egg Breakfast Quesadillas

In just 25 minutes you can be enjoying a breakfast quesadilla filled with scrambled eggs, spinach, feta cheese and red peppers.

Prep Time: 10 Minutes
Cook Time: 15 Minutes
Total Time: 25 Minutes
Serves: 5

Ingredients:

- 8 eggs (optional)
- 2 tsp olive oil
- 1 red bell pepper
- 1/2 red onion
- 1/4 cup milk
- 4 handfuls of spinach leaves
- 1 1/2 cup mozzarella cheese
- 5 sun-dried tomato tortillas
- 1/2 cup feta
- 1/4 tsp salt
- 1/4 tsp pepper
- Spray oil

Directions:

1. In a large non-stick pan over medium heat, add the olive oil
2. Once heated, add the bell pepper and onion, cook for 4-5 minutes until soft
3. In the meantime, whisk together the eggs, milk, salt and pepper in a bowl
4. Add in the egg/milk mixture into the pan with peppers and onions, stirring frequently, until eggs are almost cooked through
5. Add in the spinach and feta, fold into the eggs, stirring until spinach is wilted and eggs are cooked through
6. Remove the eggs from heat and plate
7. Spray a separate large non-stick pan with spray oil, and place over medium heat
8. Add the tortilla, on one half of the tortilla, spread about ½ cup of the egg mixture
9. Top the eggs with around ⅓ cup of shredded mozzarella cheese
10. Fold the second half of the tortilla over, then cook for 2 minutes, or until golden brown
11. Flip and cook for another minute until golden brown

12. Allow the quesadilla to cool completely, divide among the container, store for 2 days or wrap in plastic wrap and foil, and freeze for up to 2 months

To Serve: Reheat in oven at 375 for 3-5 minutes or until heated through

Nutrition Facts Per Serving (1/2 quesadilla): Calories:213 | Total Fat: 11g| Total Carbs: 15g| Protein: 15g

Mediterranean Quinoa and Feta Egg Muffins

Packed with protein and nutrients, this flavorful Mediterranean Quinoa and Feta Egg Muffins make for the perfect on-the-go breakfast.

Prep Time: 15 minutes
Cook Time: 30 minutes
Total Time: minutes
Servings: 12 muffins

Ingredients:

- 8 eggs
- 1 cup cooked quinoa
- 1 cup crumbled feta cheese
- 1/4 tsp salt
- 2 cups baby spinach finely chopped
- 1/2 cup finely chopped onion
- 1 cup chopped or sliced tomatoes, cherry or grape tomatoes
- 1/2 cup chopped and pitted Kalamata olives
- 1 tbsp chopped fresh oregano
- 2 tsp high oleic sunflower oil plus optional extra for greasing muffin tins

Directions:

1. Pre-heat oven to 350 degrees F
2. Prepare 12 silicone muffin holders on a baking sheet, or grease a 12-cup muffin tin with oil, set aside
3. In a skillet over medium heat, add the vegetable oil and onions, sauté for 2 minutes
4. Add tomatoes, sauté for another minute, then add spinach and sauté until wilted, about 1 minute
5. Remove from heat and stir in olives and oregano, set aside
6. Place the eggs in a blender or mixing bowl and blend or mix until well combined
7. Pour the eggs in to a mixing bowl (if you used a blender) then add quinoa, feta cheese, veggie mixture, and salt, and stir until well combined
8. Pour mixture in to silicone cups or greased muffin tins, dividing equally, and bake for 30 minutes, or until eggs have set and muffins are a light golden brown
9. Allow to cool completely
10. Distribute among the containers, store in fridge for 2-3 days

To Serve: Heat in the microwave for 30 seconds or until slightly heated through

Recipe Notes: Muffins can also be eaten cold. For the quinoa, I recommend making a large batch {2 cups water per each cup of dry, rinsed quinoa} and saving the extra for leftovers.

Nutritional Facts Per Serving: Calories:113 | Total Carbohydrates: 5g| Total Fat: 7g | Protein: 6g

Green Shakshuka

In this fresh twist on shakshuka, the eggs are cooked in a bed of spiced spinach and broccoli rabe instead of tomatoes. Completely different, but still tasty!

Prep Time: 25 minutes
Cook Time: 15 minutes
Total Time: 40 minutes
Servings: 2

Ingredients:

- 1 tbsp olive oil
- 1 onion, peeled and diced
- 1 clove garlic, peeled and finely minced
- 3 cups broccoli rabe, chopped
- 3 cups baby spinach leaves
- 2 tbsp whole milk or cream
- 1 tsp ground cumin
- 1/4 tsp black pepper
- 1/4 tsp salt (or to taste)
- 4 Eggs

Garnish:

- 1 pinch sea salt
- 1 pinch red pepper flakes

Directions:

- Pre-heat the oven to 350 degrees F
- Add the broccoli rabe to a large pot of boiling water, cook for 2 minutes, drain and set aside
- In a large oven-proof skillet or cast-iron pan over medium heat, add in the tablespoon of olive oil along with the diced onions, cook for about 10 minutes or until the onions become translucent
- Add the minced garlic and continue cooking for about another minute
- Cut the par-cooked broccoli rabe into small pieces, stir into the onion and garlic mixture
- Cook for a couple of minutes, then stir in the baby spinach leaves, continue to cook for a couple more minutes, stirring often, until the spinach begins to wilt
- Stir in the ground cumin, salt, ground black pepper, and milk
- Make four wells in the mixture, crack an egg into each well – be careful not to break the yolks. Also, note that it's easier to crack each egg into a small bowl and then transfer them to the pan

- Place the pan with the eggs into the pre-heated oven, cook for 10 to 15 minutes until the eggs are set to preference
- Sprinkle the cooked eggs with a dash of sea salt and a pinch of red pepper flakes
- Allow to cool, distribute among the containers, store for 2-3 days

To Serve: Microwave for 1-minute or until heated through, serve with crusty whole-wheat bread or warmed slices of pita or naan

Nutritional Facts Per Serving: Calories:278 | Carbs: 18g| Total Fat: 16g | Protein: 16g

Apple Quinoa Breakfast Bars

Start your day with these healthy apple quinoa breakfast bars that will keep you full all morning!

Prep Time: 20 Minutes
Cook Time: 40 Minutes
Total Time: 1 Hr
Serves: 12

Ingredients:

- 2 eggs
- 1 apple peeled and chopped into ½ inch chunks
- 1 cup unsweetened apple sauce
- 1 ½ cups cooked & cooled quinoa
- 1 ½ cups rolled oats
- 1/4 cup peanut butter
- 1 tsp vanilla
- 1/2 tsp cinnamon
- 1/4 cup coconut oil
- ½ tsp baking powder

Directions:

1. Heat oven to 350 degrees F
2. Spray an 8x8 inch baking dish with oil, set aside
3. In a large bowl, stir together the apple sauce, cinnamon, coconut oil, peanut butter, vanilla and eggs
4. Add in the cooked quinoa, rolled oats and baking powder, mix until completely incorporated
5. Fold in the apple chunks
6. Spread the mixture into the prepared baking dish, spreading it to each corner
7. Bake for 40 minutes, or until a toothpick comes out clean
8. Allow to cool before slicing
9. Wrap the bars individually in plastic wrap. Store in an airtight container or baggie in the freezer for up to a month.

To serve: Warm up in the oven at 350 F for 5 minutes or microwave for up to 30 seconds
Nutrition Facts Per Serving (1 bar): Calories:230 | Total Fat: 10g| Total Carbs: 31g| Protein: 7g

Mediterranean Breakfast Salad

Enjoy the ultimate Mediterranean salad for breakfast! This version is topped with cherry tomatoes, cucumbers, avocado, chopped almonds, quinoa, and herbs.

Prep Time: 5 minutes
Cook Time: 10 minutes
Total Time: 15 minutes
Servings: 2

Ingredients:

- 4 eggs (optional)
- 10 cups arugula
- 1/2 seedless cucumber, chopped
- 1 cup cooked quinoa, cooled
- 1 large avocado
- 1 cup natural almonds, chopped
- 1/2 cup mixed herbs like mint and dill, chopped
- 2 cups halved cherry tomatoes and/or heirloom tomatoes cut into wedges
- Extra virgin olive oil
- 1 lemon
- Sea salt, to taste
- Freshly ground black pepper, to taste

Directions:

1. Cook the eggs by soft-boiling them - Bring a pot of water to a boil, then reduce heat to a simmer. Gently lower all the eggs into water and allow them to simmer for 6 minutes. Remove the eggs from water and run cold water on top to stop the cooking, process set aside and peel when ready to use
2. In a large bowl, combine the arugula, tomatoes, cucumber, and quinoa
3. Divide the salad among 2 containers, store in the fridge for 2 days

To Serve: Garnish with the sliced avocado and halved egg, sprinkle herbs and almonds over top. Drizzle with olive oil, season with salt and pepper, toss to combine. Season with more salt and pepper to taste, a squeeze of lemon juice, and a drizzle of olive oil

Nutritional Facts Per Serving: Calories:252 | Carbs: 18g| Total Fat: 16g | Protein: 10g

Greek Quinoa Breakfast Bowl

Get full with this good-for-you Greek Quinoa Breakfast made with baby spinach, cherry tomatoes, and feta cheese.

Prep Time: 10 minutes
Cook Time: 20 minutes
Total Time: 30 minutes
Servings: 6

Ingredients:

- 12 eggs
- ¼ cup plain Greek yogurt
- 1 tsp onion powder
- 1 tsp granulated garlic
- ½ tsp salt
- ½ tsp pepper
- 1 tsp olive oil
- 1 (5 oz) bag baby spinach
- 1 pint cherry tomatoes, halved
- 1 cup feta cheese
- 2 cups cooked quinoa

Directions:

1. In a large bowl whisk together eggs, Greek yogurt, onion powder, granulated garlic, salt, and pepper, set aside
2. In a large skillet, heat olive oil and add spinach, cook the spinach until it is slightly wilted, about 3-4 minutes
3. Add in cherry tomatoes, cook until tomatoes are softened, 3-4 minutes
4. Stir in egg mixture and cook until the eggs are set, about 7-9 minutes, stir in the eggs as they cook to scramble
5. Once the eggs have set stir in the feta and quinoa, cook until heated through
6. Distribute evenly among the containers, store for 2-3 days

To serve: Reheat in the microwave for 30 seconds to 1 minute or heated through

Nutritional Facts Per Serving: Calories:357 | Total Carbohydrates: 8g| Total Fat: 20g | Protein: 23g

Mushroom Goat Cheese Frittata

Mushrooms, goat cheese, fresh herbs and eggs come together to create these easy and delicious frittata.

Prep Time: 15 minutes
Cook Time: 35 minutes
Total Time: 50 minutes
Servings: 4

Ingredients

- 1 tbsp olive oil
- 1 small onion, diced
- 10 oz crimini or your favorite mushrooms, sliced
- 1 garlic clove, minced
- 10 eggs
- 2/3 cup half and half
- 1/4 cup fresh chives, minced
- 2 tsp fresh thyme, minced
- 1/2 tsp kosher salt
- 1/2 tsp black pepper
- 4 oz goat cheese

Directions:

1. Preheat the oven to 375 degrees F
2. In an over safe skillet or cast-iron pan over medium heat, olive oil
3. Add in the onion and sauté for 3-5 mins until golden
4. Add in the sliced mushrooms and garlic, continue to sauté until mushrooms are golden brown, about 10-12 minutes
5. In a large bowl, whisk together the eggs, half and half, chives, thyme, salt and pepper
6. Place the goat cheese over the mushroom mixture and pour the egg mixture over the top
7. Stir the mixture in the pan and cook over medium heat until the edges are set but the center is still loose, about 8-10 minutes
8. Put the pan in the oven and finish cooking for an additional 8-10 minutes or until set
9. Allow to cool completely before slicing
10. Wrap the slices in plastic wrap and then aluminum foil and place in the freezer.

To Serve: Remove the aluminum foil and plastic wrap, and microwave for 2 minutes, then allow to rest for 30 seconds, enjoy!

Nutritional Facts Per Serving: Calories:243 | Total Carbohydrates: 5g| Total Fat: 17g | Protein: 15g

Greek Yogurt Breakfast Bowl

Quick to make and yummy, this Greek Yogurt Breakfast Bowl is topped with pomegranate seeds and honey.

Prep Time: 5 minutes
Total Time: 5 minutes
Servings: 1

Ingredients:

- 1 cup Greek Yogurt plain
- 1/3 cup Pomegranate Seeds (or fresh fruit of your choice)
- 1 tsp honey

Directions:

1. In a jar with a lid, add the Greek yogurt in a bowl top with fruit and drizzle honey over the top
2. Close the lid and refrigerate for 2-3 days

Nutritional Facts Per Serving: Calories:116 | Carbs: 24g| Total Fat: 1.2g | Protein: 4g

Vegetable Breakfast Bowl

This awesome Veggie Breakfast Bowl is filled with flavorful vegetables and topped with a zesty lemon dressing!

Prep Time: 25 minutes
Cook Time: 5 minutes
Total Time: 30 minutes
Servings: 2

Ingredients:

Breakfast Bowl:

- 1 ½ cups cooked quinoa
- 1 lb asparagus[1], cut into bite-sized pieces, ends trimmed and discarded
- 1 tbsp avocado oil or olive oil
- 3 cups shredded kale leaves
- 1 batch lemony dressing
- 3 cups shredded, uncooked Brussels sprouts
- 1 avocado, peeled, pitted and thinly-sliced
- 4 eggs, cooked to your preference (optional)

Garnishes:

- Toasted sesame seeds
- Crushed red pepper
- Sunflower seeds
- Sliced almonds
- Hummus

Lemon Dressing:

- 2 tsp Dijon mustard
- 1 garlic clove, minced
- 2 tbsp avocado oil or olive oil
- 2 tbsp freshly-squeezed lemon juice
- Salt, to taste
- Freshly-cracked black pepper, to taste

Directions:

1. In a large sauté pan over medium-high heat, add the oil
2. Once heated, add the asparagus and sauté for 4-5 minutes, stirring occasionally, until tender. Remove from heat and set side
3. Add the Brussels sprouts, quinoa, and cooked asparagus, and toss until combined
4. Distribute among the container, store in fridge for 2-3 days

To serve: In a large, mixing bowl combine the kale and lemony dressing. Use your fingers to massage the dressing into the kale for 2-3 minutes, or until the leaves are dark and softened, set aside. In a small mixing bowl, combine the avocado, lemon juice, dijon mustard, garlic clove, salt, and pepper. Assemble the bowls by smearing a spoonful of hummus along the side of each bowl, then portion the kale salad evenly between the four bowls. Top with the avocado slices, egg, and your desired garnishes

Recipe Note: Feel free to sub the asparagus with your favorite vegetable(s), sautéing or roasting them until cooked

Nutritional Facts Per Serving: Calories:632 | Carbs: 52g| Total Fat: 39g | Protein: 24g

Mediterranean Breakfast Burrito

Meatless and easy to make, these healthy breakfast burritos are full of Mediterranean flavors!

Prep Time: 15 minutes
Cook Time: 5 minutes
Total Time: 20 minutes
Servings: 6 burritos

Ingredients:

- 9 eggs whole
- 6 tortillas whole 10 inch, regular or sun-dried tomato
- 3 tbsp sun-dried tomatoes, chopped
- 1/2 cup feta cheese I use light/low-fat feta
- 2 cups baby spinach washed and dried
- 3 tbsp black olives, sliced
- 3/4 cup refried beans, canned

Garnish:

- Salsa

Directions:

1. Spray a medium frying pan with non- stick spray, add the eggs and scramble and toss for about 5 minutes, or until eggs are no longer liquid
2. Add in the spinach, black olives, sun-dried tomatoes and continue to stir and toss until no longer wet
3. Add in the feta cheese and cover, cook until cheese is melted
4. Add 2 tbsp of refried beans to each tortilla
5. Top with egg mixture, dividing evenly between all burritos, and wrap
6. Frying in a pan until lightly browned
7. Allow to cool completely before slicing
8. Wrap the slices in plastic wrap and then aluminum foil and place in the freezer for up to 2 months or fridge for 2 days

To Serve: Remove the aluminum foil and plastic wrap, and microwave for 2 minutes, then allow to rest for 30 seconds, enjoy! Enjoy hot with salsa and fruit

Nutritional Facts Per Serving: Calories:252 | Total Carbohydrates: 21g| Total Fat: 11g | Protein: 14g |

Quinoa Granola

Naturally sweet, you'll love having this healthy protein-packed granola for breakfast!

Prep Time: 5 Minutes

Cook Time: 25 Minutes

Total Time: 30 Minutes

Ingredients:

- 1 cup Old-Fashioned rolled oats, or gluten-free
- 1/2 cup uncooked white quinoa
- 2 cups raw almonds, roughly chopped
- 1 Tbsp coconut sugar or sub organic brown sugar, muscovado, or organic cane sugar
- 1 pinch sea salt
- 3 1/2 tbsp coconut oil
- 1/4 cup maple syrup or agave nectar

Directions:

1. Preheat oven to 340 degrees F
2. In a large mixing bowl, add the quinoa, almonds, oats, coconut sugar, and salt, stir to combine
3. To a small saucepan, add the maple syrup and coconut oil, warm over medium heat for 2-3 minutes, whisking frequently until completely mixed and combined
4. Immediately pour over the dry ingredients, stir to combine and thoroughly all oats and nuts
5. Arrange on a large baking sheet, spread into an even layer
6. Bake for 20 minutes
7. Then remove from oven, stir and toss the granola - make sure to turn the pan around so the other end goes into the oven first and bakes evenly
8. Bake for 5-10 minutes more - watch carefully so it doesn't burn and it's golden brown and very fragrant
9. Allow to cool completely, then store in a container for up to 7 days

Nutritional Facts Per Serving: Calories:332 | Total Carbohydrates: 30g| Total Fat: 20g | Protein: 9g

Cappuccino Muffins

Rich in deep coffee flavor and chocolate chips, these muffins are perfect for breakfast or brunch.

Prep Time: 30 Minutes
Cook Time: 20 Minutes
Total Time: 50 Minutes

Ingredients:

- 2 1/3 cups all-purpose flour
- 2 tsp baking powder
- 1 tsp salt
- 1 tsp ground cinnamon
- ¾ cup hot water
- 2 tbsp espresso powder or instant coffee
- 2 eggs
- 1 cup sugar
- ¾ cup vegetable oil
- 1/3 cup mini chocolate chips
- ¼ cup milk

Directions:

1. Preheat oven to 425 degree F
2. In a medium bowl, whisk together the flour, baking powder, salt and cinnamon, set aside
3. In a small bowl, combine the hot water and espresso powder, stir to dissolve, add milk, stir to combine and set aside
4. In a large bowl, whisk together eggs, sugar and oil, slowly add the coffee mixture, and stir to combine Then add in the dry ingredients in thirds, whisking gently until smooth
5. Add in the chocolate chips, stir to combine
6. Place the muffin papers in a 12-cup muffin tin
7. Fill each cup half way
8. Bake for 17-20 minutes, until risen and set
9. Allow to cool completely before slicing
10. Wrap the slices in plastic wrap and then aluminum foil and store in fridge for up to 4-5 days

To Serve: Remove the aluminum foil and plastic wrap, and microwave for 2 minutes, then allow to rest for 30 seconds, enjoy!

Nutritional Facts Per Serving (1 muffin): Calories:201 | Carbs: 29g| Total Fat: 8g | Protein: 2g

Main Entrées

Mediterranean Zucchini Noodles

Swap out traditional noodles and lighten up "pasta night" with this recipe for Mediterranean Zucchini Noodles. This simple dinner combines cherry tomatoes, sun-dried tomatoes and artichoke hearts.

Prep Time: 10 Minutes
Cook Time: 10 Minutes
Total Time: 20 Minutes
Serves: 2

Ingredients:

- 2 large zucchini or 1 package of store-bought zucchini noodles
- 1 tsp olive oil
- 4 cloves garlic diced
- 10 oz cherry tomatoes cut in half
- 2-4 oz plain hummus
- 1 tsp oregano
- 1/2 tsp red wine vinegar plus more to taste
- 1/2 cup jarred artichoke hearts, drained and chopped
- 1/4 cup sun-dried tomatoes, drained and chopped
- Salt, to taste
- Pepper to taste
- Parmesan and fresh basil for topping

Directions:

1. Prepare the zucchini by cutting of the ends off zucchini and spiralize, set aside
2. In a pan over medium heat, add in olive oil
3. Then add in the garlic and cherry tomatoes to the pan, sauté until tomatoes begin to burst, about 3 to 4 minutes
4. Add in the zucchini noodles, sun-dried tomatoes, hummus, oregano, artichoke hearts and red wine vinegar to the pan, sauté for 1-2 minutes, or until zucchini is tender-crisp and heated through
5. Season to taste with salt and pepper as needed
6. Allow the zoodle to cool
7. Distribute among the containers, store in the fridge for 2-3 days

To Serve: Reheat in the microwave for 30 seconds or until heated through, serve immediately with parmesan and fresh basil. Enjoy

Nutritional Facts Per Serving: Calories:241 | Carbs: 8g| Total Fat: 37g | Protein: 10g

Lemon Herb Avocado Chicken Salad

This Lemon Herb Avocado Chicken Salad is amazing! It's made with crispy bacon & creamy feta cheese and features a fresh homemade dressing!

Prep Time: 10 Minutes
Cook Time: 15 Minutes
Total Time: 25 Minutes
Serves: 4

Ingredients:

Marinade/ Dressing:

- 2 tbsp olive oil
- 1/4 cup fresh lemon juice
- 2 tbsp water
- 2 tbsp fresh chopped parsley
- 2 tsp garlic, minced
- 1 tsp each dried thyme and dried rosemary
- 1 tsp salt
- 1/4 tsp cracked pepper, or to taste
- 1 pound skinless & boneless chicken thigh fillets or chicken breasts

Salad:

- 4 cups Romaine lettuce leaves, washed and dried
- 1 large avocado, pitted, peeled and sliced
- 8 oz feta cheese
- 1 cup grape tomatoes, halved
- 1/4 of a red onion, sliced, optional
- 1/4 cup diced bacon, trimmed of rind and fat (optional)
- Lemon wedges, to serve

Directions:

1. In a large jug, whisk together the olive oil, lemon juice, water, chopped parsley, garlic, thyme, rosemary, salt, and pepper
2. Pour half of the marinade into a large, shallow dish and refrigerate the remaining marinade to use as the dressing
3. Add the chicken to the marinade in the bowl, allow the chicken to marinade for 15-30 minutes (or up to two hours in the refrigerator if you can)
4. In the meantime,
5. Once the chicken is ready, place a skillet or grill over medium-high heat add 1 tbsp of oil in, sear the chicken on both sides until browned and cooked through about 7 minutes per side, depending on thickness, and discard of the marinade

6. Allow the chicken to rest for 5 minutes, slice and then allow the chicken to cool
7. Distribute among the containers, and keep in the refrigerator

To Serve: Reheat the chicken in the microwave for 30 seconds to 1 minutes. In a bowl, add the romaine lettuce, avocado, feta cheese, grape tomatoes, red onion and bacon, mix to combine. Arrange the chicken over salad. Drizzle the salad with the Untouched dressing. Serve with lemon wedges and enjoy!

Nutritional Facts Per Serving: Calories:378 | Carbs: 6g| Total Fat: 22g | Protein: 31g

Mediterranean Avocado Salmon Salad

Loaded with cucumbers, olives, tomatoes, and feta cheese, this Avocado Salmon Salad is incredible!

Prep Time: 10 Minutes
Cook Time: 10 Minutes
Total Time: 20 Minutes
Serves: 4

Ingredients:
- 1 lb skinless salmon fillets

Marinade/Dressing:
- 3 tbsp olive oil
- 2 tbsp lemon juice fresh, squeezed
- 1 tbsp red wine vinegar, optional
- 1 tbsp fresh chopped parsley
- 2 tsp garlic minced
- 1 tsp dried oregano
- 1 tsp salt
- Cracked pepper, to taste

Salad:
- 4 cups Romaine (or Cos) lettuce leaves, washed and dried
- 1 large cucumber, diced
- 2 Roma tomatoes, diced
- 1 red onion, sliced
- 1 avocado, sliced
- 1/2 cup feta cheese crumbled
- 1/3 cup pitted Kalamata olives or black olives, sliced
- Lemon wedges to serve

Directions:
1. In a jug, whisk together the olive oil, lemon juice, red wine vinegar, chopped parsley, garlic minced, oregano, salt and pepper
2. Pour out half of the marinade into a large, shallow dish, refrigerate the remaining marinade to use as the dressing
3. Coat the salmon in the rest of the marinade
4. Place a skillet pan or grill over medium-high, add 1 tbsp oil and sear salmon on both sides until crispy and cooked through
5. Allow the salmon to cool
6. Distribute the salmon among the containers, store in the fridge for 2-3 days

To Serve: Prepare the salad by placing the romaine lettuce, cucumber, roma tomatoes, red onion, avocado, feta cheese, and olives in a large salad bowl. Reheat the salmon in the microwave for 30seconds to 1 minute or until heated through. Slice the salmon and arrange over salad. Drizzle the salad with the remaining untouched dressing, serve with lemon wedges.

Nutritional Facts Per Serving: Calories:411 | Carbs: 12g| Total Fat: 27g | Protein: 28g

One Skillet Greek Lemon Chicken and Rice

Made entirely in one pan, this Greek lemon chicken dish is completely packed with classic Greek flavors!

Prep Time: 10 Minutes
Cook Time: 45 Minutes
Total Time: 55 Minutes
Serves: 5

Ingredients:

Marinade:

- 2 tsp dried oregano
- 1 tsp dried minced onion
- 4-5 cloves garlic, minced
- Zest of 1 lemon
- 1/2 tsp kosher salt
- 1/2 tsp black pepper
- 1-2 Tbsp olive oil to make a loose paste
- 5 bone-in, skin on chicken thighs

Rice:

- 1 1/2 Tbsp olive oil
- 1 large yellow onion, peeled and diced
- 1 cup dry long-grain white rice (NOT minute or quick cooking varieties)
- 2 cups chicken stock
- 1 1/4 tsp dried oregano
- 5 cloves garlic, minced
- 3/4 tsp kosher salt
- 1/2 tsp black pepper
- Lemon slices, optional
- Fresh minced parsley, for garnish
- Extra lemon zest, for garnish

Directions:

1. In a large resealable plastic bag, add the oregano, dried minced onion, garlic, lemon zest, salt, black pepper, and olive oil, massage to combine
2. Add chicken thighs, and then turn/massage to coat, refrigerate 15 minutes or overnight
3. Preheat oven to 350 F degrees
4. In a large cast iron or heavy oven safe skillet over medium-high heat, add 1 1/2 Tbsp olive oil to

5. Remove the chicken thighs from the refrigerator, shake off the excess marinade and add chicken thighs, skin side down, to pan, cook 4-5 minutes per side

6. Transfer to a plate and wipe the skillet lightly with a paper towel to remove any burnt bits, reserving chicken grease in pan.

7. Lower the heat to medium and add onion to pan, cook 3-4 minutes, until softened and slightly charred. Add in garlic and cook 1 minute

8. Then add in the rice, oregano, salt and pepper, stir together and cook for 1 minute

9. Pour in chicken stock, turn the temperature up to medium-high, bring to a simmer

10. Once simmering, place the chicken thighs on top of the rice mixture, push down gently

11. Cover with lid or foil, and bake 35 minutes

12. Uncover, return to oven and bake an additional 10-15 minutes, until liquid is removed, the rice is tender, and chicken is cooked through

13. Allow the rice and chicken to cool

14. Distribute among the containers, store in fridge for 2-3 days

To serve: Reheat in the microwave for 1 minute to 2 minutes or cooked through. Garnish with lemon zest and parsley, and serve!

Nutritional Facts Per Serving: Calories:325 | Carbs: 35g| Total Fat: 11g | Protein: 21g

Italian Chicken with Sweet Potato and Broccoli

Have Italian baked chicken with sweet potatoes and broccoli ready in just 45 minutes with this easy recipe!

Prep Time: 15 Minutes
Cook Time: 30 Minutes
Total Time: 45 Minutes
Serves: 8

Ingredients:

- 2 lbs boneless skinless chicken breasts, cut into small pieces
- 5-6 cups broccoli florets
- 3 tbsp Italian seasoning mix of your choice
- a few tbsp of olive oil
- 3 sweet potatoes, peeled and diced
- Coarse sea salt, to taste
- Freshly cracked pepper, to taste

Toppings:

- Avocado
- Lemon juice
- Chives
- Olive oil, for serving

Directions:

1. Preheat the oven to 425 degrees F
2. Toss the chicken pieces with the Italian seasoning mix and a drizzle of olive oil, stir to combine then store in the fridge for about 30 minutes
3. Arrange the broccoli florets and sweet potatoes on a sheet pan, drizzle with the olive oil, sprinkle generously with salt
4. Arrange the chicken on a separate sheet pan
5. Bake both in the oven for 12-15 minutes
6. Transfer the chicken and broccoli to a plate, toss the sweet potatoes and continue to roast for another 15 minutes, or until ready
7. Allow the chicken, broccoli, and sweet potatoes to cool
8. Distribute among the containers and store for 2-3 days

To Serve: Reheat in the microwave for 1 minute or until heated through, top with the topping of choice. Enjoy

Recipe Notes: Any kind of vegetables work will with this recipe! So, add favorites like carrots, brussels sprouts and asparagus.

Nutrition Facts Per Serving: Calories:222 | Total Fat: 4.9g| Total Carbs: 15.3g | Protein: 28g

Roasted Vegetable Flatbread

Topped with cheese, herbs, and fresh veggies, this vibrant Roasted Vegetable Flatbread makes for an amazing lunch or dinner!

Prep Time: 20 Minutes
Cook Time: 25 Minutes
Total Time: 45 Minutes
Serves: 12 Slices

Ingredients:

- 16 oz pizza dough, homemade or frozen
- 6 oz soft goat cheese, divided
- ¾ cup grated Parmesan cheese divided
- 3 tbsp chopped fresh dill, divided
- 1 small red onion, sliced thinly
- 1 small zucchini, sliced thinly
- 2 small tomatoes, thinly sliced
- 1 small red pepper, thinly sliced into rings
- Olive oil
- Salt, to taste
- Pepper, to taste

Directions:

1. Preheat the oven to 400 degrees F
2. Roll the dough into a large rectangle, and then place it on a piece of parchment paper sprayed with non-stick spray
3. Take a knife and spread half the goat cheese onto one half of the dough, then sprinkle with half the dill and half the Parmesan cheese
4. Carefully fold the other half of the dough on top of the cheese, spread and sprinkle the remaining parmesan and goat cheese
5. Layer the thinly sliced vegetables over the top
6. Brush the olive oil over the top of the veggies and sprinkle with salt, pepper, and the remaining dill
7. Bake for 22-25 minutes, until the edges are medium brown, cut in half, lengthwise
8. Then slice the flatbread in long 2-inch slices and allow to cool
9. Distribute among the containers, store for 2 days

To Serve: Reheat in the oven at 375 degrees for 5 minutes or until hot. Enjoy with a fresh salad.

Nutritional Facts Per Serving: Calories:170 | Carbs: 21g| Total Fat: 6g | Protein: 8g

Mediterranean Chicken Pasta Bake

Cheesy and full of Mediterranean flavor, this chicken pasta bake has a delicious sauce you'll love!

Prep Time: 1 Hour
Cook Time: 30 Minutes
Total Time: 1 H 30 Minutes
Serves: 4

Ingredients:

Marinade:

- 1½ lbs. boneless, skinless chicken thighs, cut into bite-sized pieces*
- 2 garlic cloves, thinly sliced
- 2-3 tbsp. marinade from artichoke hearts
- 4 sprigs of fresh oregano, leaves stripped
- Olive oil
- Red wine vinegar

Pasta Bake:

- 1 lb whole wheat fusilli pasta
- 1 red onion, thinly sliced
- 1 pint grape or cherry tomatoes, whole
- ½ cup marinated artichoke hearts, roughly chopped
- ½ cup white beans, rinsed + drained (I use northern white beans)
- ½ cup Kalamata olives, roughly chopped
- ⅓ cup parsley and basil leaves, roughly chopped
- 2-3 handfuls of part-skim shredded mozzarella cheese
- Salt, to taste
- Pepper, to taste

Garnish:

- Parsley
- Basil leaves

Directions:

1. Create the chicken marinade by drain the artichoke hearts reserving the juice
2. In a large bowl, add the artichoke juice, garlic, chicken, and oregano leaves, drizzle with olive oil, a splash of red wine vinegar, and mix well to coat
3. Marinate for at least 1 hour, maximum 3 hours
4. Cook the pasta in boiling salted water, drain and set aside
5. Preheat your oven to 425 degrees F

6. In a casserole dish, add the sliced onions and tomatoes, toss with olive oil, salt and pepper. Then cook, stirring occasionally, until the onions are soft and the tomatoes start to burst, about 15-20 minutes
7. In the meantime, in a large skillet over medium heat, add 1 tsp of olive oil
8. Remove the chicken from the marinade, pat dry, and season with salt and pepper
9. Working in batches, brown the chicken on both sides, leaving slightly undercooked
10. Remove the casserole dish from the oven, add in the cooked pasta, browned chicken, artichoke hearts, beans, olives, and chopped herbs, stir to combine
11. Top with grated cheese
12. Bake for an additional 5-7 minutes, until the cheese is brown and bubbling
13. Remove from the oven and allow the dish to cool completely
14. Distribute among the containers, store for 2-3 days

To Serve: Reheat in the microwave for 1-2 minutes or until heated through.
Garnish with fresh herbs and serve

Nutritional Facts Per Serving: Calories:487 | Carbs: 95g| Total Fat: 5g | Protein: 22g

Garlic Marinated Chicken

Full of flavor, this garlic marinated chicken with roasted vegetables is super delicious and healthy!

Prep Time: 45 minutes
Cook Time: 15 minutes
Total Time: 1 hour
Serves: 3

Ingredients:

- 1 ½ lbs. boneless skinless chicken breasts,
- 1/4 cup olive oil
- 1/4 cup lemon juice
- 3 cloves garlic, minced
- 1/2 tbsp dried oregano
- 1/2 tsp salt
- Freshly cracked pepper

To Serve:

- Rice or cauliflower rice
- Roasted vegetables, such as carrots, asparagus, or green beans

Directions:

1. In a large Ziplock bag or dish, add in the olive oil, lemon juice, garlic, oregano, salt, and pepper
2. Close the bag and shake the ingredients to combine, or stir the ingredients in the dish until well combined
3. Filet each chicken breast into two thinner pieces and place the pieces in the bag or dish - make sure the chicken is completely covered in marinade and allow to marinate for up to 30 minutes up to 8 hours, turn occasionally to maximize the marinade flavors
4. Once ready, heat a large skillet over medium heat
5. Once heated, transfer the chicken from the marinade to the hot skillet and cook on each side cooked through, about 5-7 minutes each side, depending on the size - Discard of any excess marinade
6. Transfer the cooked chicken from the skillet to a clean cutting board, allow to rest for five minutes before slicing
7. Distribute the chicken, cooked rice and vegetables among the containers. Store in the fridge for up to 4 days.

To Serve: Reheat in the microwave for 1-2 minutes or until heated through and enjoy!

Nutrition Facts Per Serving: Calories:446 | Total Fat: 24g| Total Carbs: 4g| Fiber: 0g| Protein: 52g

Mediterranean Steamed Salmon with Fresh Herbs and Lemon

This Mediterranean-style steamed salmon is made with fresh herbs, garlic, and lemon and is the perfect quick dinner!

Prep Time: 10 Minutes
Cook Time: 15 Minutes
Total Time: 25 Minutes
Serves: 4

Ingredients:

- 1 yellow onion, halved and sliced
- 4 green onions spring onions, trimmed and sliced lengthwise, divided
- 1 lb skin-on salmon fillet (such as wild Alaskan), cut into 4 portions
- 1/2 tsp Aleppo pepper
- 4 to 5 garlic cloves, chopped
- Extra virgin olive oil
- A large handful fresh parsley
- 1 lemon, thinly sliced
- 1 tsp ground coriander
- 1 tsp ground cumin
- 1/2 cup white wine (or you can use water or low-sodium broth, if you prefer) Kosher salt, to taste
- Black pepper, to taste

Directions:

1. Prepare a large piece of wax paper or parchment paper (about 2 feet long) and place it right in the center of a 10-inch deep pan or braiser
2. Place the sliced yellow onions and a sprinkle a little bit of green onions the onions on the bottom of the braiser
3. Arrange the salmon, skin-side down, on top, season with kosher salt and black pepper
4. In a small bowl, mix together the coriander, cumin, and Aleppo pepper, coat top of salmon with the spice mixture, and drizzle with a little bit of extra virgin olive oil
5. Then add garlic, parsley and the remaining green onions on top of the salmon (make sure that everything is arrange evenly over the salmon portions.)
6. Arrange the lemon slices on top of the salmon
7. Add another drizzle of extra virgin olive oil, then add the white wine
8. Fold the parchment paper over to cover salmon, secure the edges and cover the braiser with the lid
9. Place the braising pan over medium-high heat, cook for 5 minutes

10. Lower the heat to medium, cook for another 8 minutes, covered still
11. Remove from heat and allow to rest undisturbed for about 5 minutes.
12. Remove the lid and allow the salmon to cool completely
13. Distribute among the containers, store for 2-3 days

To Serve: Reheat in the microwave for 1-2 minutes or until heated through.

Recipe Notes: The pan or braiser you use needs to have a lid to allow the steamed salmon.

Nutritional Facts Per Serving: Calories:321 | Carbs: g| Total Fat: 18g | Protein: 28g

Seafood Paella

This Mediterranean paella is super easy to create and filled with yummy shrimp and lobster!

Prep Time: 20 Minutes
Cook Time: 40 Minutes
Total Time: 60 Minutes
Serves: 4-5

Ingredients:

- 4 small lobster tails (6-12 oz each)
- Water
- 3 tbsp Extra Virgin Olive Oil
- 1 large yellow onion, chopped
- 2 cups Spanish rice or short grain rice, soaked in water for 15 minutes and then drained
- 4 garlic cloves, chopped
- 2 large pinches of Spanish saffron threads soaked in 1/2 cup water
- 1 tsp Sweet Spanish paprika
- 1 tsp cayenne pepper
- 1/2 tsp aleppo pepper flakes
- Salt, to taste
- 2 large Roma tomatoes, finely chopped
- 6 oz French green beans, trimmed
- 1 lb prawns or large shrimp or your choice, peeled and deveined
- 1/4 cup chopped fresh parsley

Directions:

1. In a large pot, add 3 cups of water and bring it to a rolling boil
2. Add in the lobster tails and allow boil briefly, about 1-2 minutes or until pink, remove from heat
3. Using tongs transfer the lobster tails to a plate and Do not discard the lobster cooking water
4. Allow the lobster is cool, then remove the shell and cut into large chunks.
5. In a large deep pan or skillet over medium-high heat, add 3 tbsp olive oil
6. Add the chopped onions, sauté the onions for 2 minutes and then add the rice, and cook for 3 more minutes, stirring regularly
7. Then add in the lobster cooking water and the chopped garlic and, stir in the saffron and its soaking liquid, cayenne pepper, aleppo pepper, paprika, and salt

8. Gently stir in the chopped tomatoes and green beans, bring to a boil and allow the liquid slightly reduce, then cover (with lid or tightly wrapped foil) and cook over low heat for 20 minutes

9. Once done, uncover and spread the shrimp over the rice, push it into the rice slightly, add in a little water, if needed

10. Cover and cook for another 10-15 minutes until the shrimp turn pink

11. Then add in the cooked lobster chunks

12. Once the lobster is warmed through, remove from heat allow the dish to cool completely

13. Distribute among the containers, store for 2 days

To Serve: Reheat in the microwave for 1-2 minutes or until heated through. Garnish with parsley and enjoy!

Recipe Notes: Remember to soak your rice if needed to help with the cooking process

Nutritional Facts Per Serving: Calories:536 | Carbs: 56g| Total Fat: 26g | Protein: 50g

Mediterranean Pasta Salad

Made with fresh arugula, veggies, and chicken salad, this delicious Mediterranean inspired pasta dish is finished with an amazing lemon vinaigrette you have to try!

Prep Time: 25 Minutes

Total Time: 25 Minutes

Serves: 8

Ingredients:

Salad:

- 8 oz pasta, I used farfalle, any smallish pasta works great!
- 1 cup rotisserie chicken, chopped
- 1/2 cup sun-dried tomatoes packed in oil, drained and coarsely chopped
- 1/2 cup jarred marinated artichoke hearts, drained and coarsely chopped
- 1/2 of 1 full English cucumber, chopped
- 1/3 cup kalamata olives, coarsely chopped
- 2 cups lightly packed fresh arugula
- 1/4 cup fresh flat leaf Italian parsley, coarsely chopped
- 1 small avocado, pit removed and coarsely chopped
- 1/3 cup feta cheese

Dressing:

- 4 tbsp red wine vinegar
- 1 ½ tbsp dijon mustard, do not use regular mustard
- 1/2 tsp dried oregano
- 1 tsp dried basil
- 1 clove garlic, minced
- 1-2 tsp honey
- 1/2 cup olive oil
- 3 tbsp freshly squeezed lemon juice
- Fine sea salt, to taste
- Freshly cracked pepper, to taste

Directions:

1. Prepare the pasta according to package directions until al dente, drain the pasta and allow it to completely cool to room temperature, then add it to a large bowl
2. Add in the chopped rotisserie chicken, chopped cucumber, coarsely chopped kalamata olives, coarsely chopped sun-dried tomatoes, coarsely chopped artichoke hearts, arugula, and parsley, toss
3. Distribute the salad among the containers, store for 2-3 days

4. Prepare the dressing - In a mason jar with a lid, combine the red wine vinegar, Dijon mustard, garlic, 1/2 teaspoon salt (or to taste), dried oregano, dried basil and 1/4 teaspoon pepper (or to taste, honey (add to sweetness preference), olive oil, and freshly squeezed lemon juice, place the lid on the mason jar and shake to combine, store in fridge

To Serve: Add in the avocado and feta cheese to the salad, drizzle with the dressing, adjust any seasonings salt and pepper to taste, serve

Nutritional Facts Per Serving: Calories:326 | Carbs: 24g| Total Fat: 21g | Protein: 8g

Roasted Vegetable Quinoa Bowl

This quick and easy roasted veggie bowl is created with just 5 delicious ingredients: Chili-lime kale, quinoa, garlic roasted broccoli, spicy roasted chickpeas, and curry roasted sweet potatoes!

Prep Time: 10 Minutes
Cook Time: 20 Minutes
Total Time: 30 Minutes
Serves: 2

Ingredients:

Quinoa:

- ¾ cup quinoa, rinsed
- 1 ½ cups vegetable broth
- Chili-Lime Kale
- 1/2 tsp chili powder
- pinch salt
- pinch pepper
- 2 cups packed kale, de-stemmed and chopped
- 1 tsp olive, coconut or canola oil
- Juice of 1/4 lime

Garlic Roasted Broccoli:

- 2 cups broccoli,
- 2 tsp olive or canola oil
- 2 cloves garlic, minced
- Pinch of salt
- Black pepper

Curry Roasted Sweet Potatoes:

- 1 small sweet potato
- 1 tsp olive or canola oil
- 1 tsp curry powder
- 1 tsp sriracha
- Pinch salt

Spicy Roasted Chickpeas:

- 1 ½ cups (cooked) chickpeas
- 1 tsp olive or canola oil
- 2 tsp sriracha
- 2 tsp soy sauce

Optional:

- Lime
- Avocado
- Hummus
- Red pepper flakes
- Guacamole

Directions:

1. Preheat the oven to 400-degree F
2. Line a large baking sheet with parchment paper
3. Prepare the vegetables by chopping the broccoli into medium sized florets, de-stemming and chopping the kale, scrubbing and slicing the sweet potato into ¼" wide rounds
4. Take the broccoli florets and massage with oil, garlic, salt and pepper - making sure to work the ingredients into the tops of each florets - Place the florets in a row down in the center third of a large baking sheet
5. Using the same bowl, the broccoli in, mix together the chickpeas, oil, sriracha and soy sauce, then spread them out in a row next to the broccoli
6. In the same bowl combine the oil, curry powder, salt, and sriracha, add the sliced sweet potato and toss to coat, then lay the rounds on the remaining third of the baking tray
7. Bake for 10 minutes, flip the sweet potatoes and broccoli, and redistribute the chickpeas to cook evenly Bake for another 8-12 minutes
8. For the Quinoa: Prepare the quinoa by rinsing and draining it. Add the rinsed quinoa and vegetable broth to a small saucepan and bring to a boil over high heat. Turn the heat down to medium-low, cover and allow to simmer for about 15 minutes. Once cooked, fluff with a fork and set aside
9. In the meantime, place a large skillet with 1 tsp oil, add in the kale and cook for about 5 minutes, or until nearly tender
10. Add in the salt, chili powder, and lime juice, toss to coat and cook for another 2-3 minutes
11. Allow all the ingredient to cool
12. Distribute among the containers – Add ½ to 1 cup of quinoa into each bowl, top with ½ of the broccoli, ½ kale, ½ the chickpeas and ½ sweet potatoes

To Serve: Reheat in the microwave for 1-2 minutes or until heated through. Enjoy

Nutritional Facts Per Serving: Calories:611 | Carbs: 93g| Total Fat: 17g | Protein: 24g

Grilled Salmon Tzatziki Bowl

In just 30 minutes you'll be enjoying grilled salmon with a nice tzatziki over your favorite vegetables and grains!

Prep Time: 15 Minutes
Cook Time: 15 Minutes
Total Time: 30 Minutes
Serves: 2

Ingredients:

- 8–10 ounces salmon, serves 2
- Olive oil for brushing
- Salt and pepper
- 1 lemon- sliced in half

Tzatziki:

- ½ cup plain yogurt
- ½ cup sour cream
- 1 garlic clove- finely minced
- 1 tbsp lemon juice, more to taste
- 1 tbsp olive oil
- ½ tsp kosher salt
- ¼ tsp white pepper or black
- ⅛ cup fresh chopped dill (or mint, cilantro or Italian parsley – or a mix)
- 1 ½ cups finely sliced or diced cucumber

Optional Bowl Additions:

- Cooked Quinoa or rice
- Arugula or other greens
- Grilled veggies like eggplant, peppers, tomatoes, or zucchini
- Fresh veggies of your choice - radishes, cucumber, tomatoes, sprouts
- Garnish with olive oil, lemon, and fresh herbs

Directions:

1. Preheat heat grill to medium high
2. Cook 1 cup quinoa or rice on the stove, according to directions, allow to cool
3. Brush the salmon with olive oil, season with salt and pepper, set aside
4. Create the Tzatziki, by adding plain yogurt, sour cream, garlic clove, lemon juice, olive oil, kosher salt, and white pepper in a bowl, taste and add more lemon juice if desired, store in fridge
5. Place the salmon on the grill, along with the veggies of you choose to grill, brushing all with olive oil, salt and pepper

6. Grill the salmon on both sides for 3-4 minutes, or until cooked through
7. Then grill the lemon, open side down, until good grill marks appear
8. Once the veggies and salmon are done, allow them to cool
9. Distribute among the containers - Divide quinoa among the containers, arrange the grilled vegetables and salmon over top.

To Serve: Reheat in the microwave for 1 minute or until heated through. Top with the greens and the fresh veggies, then drizzle a little olive oil on top and season with salt, squeeze the grilled lemon over the whole bowl, spoon the tzatziki over top the salmon, sprinkle with the fresh dill or other herbs. Enjoy with a glass of wine.

Nutritional Facts Per Serving: Calories:458 | Carbs: 29g| Total Fat: 24g | Protein: 30g

Italian Sausage and Veggie Pizza Pasta

Just wait until you try this Italian Sausage and Veggie Pizza Pasta!

Prep Time: 10 Minutes

Cook Time: 30 Minutes

Total Time: 40 Minutes

Serves: 8

Ingredients:

- 1 tsp olive oil
- 1 (2.25 oz) can of sliced black olives
- 1 (28 oz) can of tomato sauce
- 1 (16 oz) box penne pasta
- 3 cups water
- 3 sweet Italian sausage links, casings removed, around 1 lb of sausage
- 1 cup sliced onions
- 1 cup sliced green bell pepper
- 2-3 garlic cloves, minced or pressed
- 8 oz. sliced mushrooms
- 1/2 cup Pepperoni, cut in half and then each half cut into thirds + a few extra whole pieces for topping
- 1/2 tsp Italian seasoning
- 1/2 tsp salt
- Salt, to taste
- Pepper to taste
- 2 cups shredded mozzarella cheese, divided

Garnish:

- Chopped fresh parsley and Romano cheese

Directions:

1. In a deep heavy-bottom, oven-safe pot over medium heat, add the oil
2. Once heated, add in the sausage and break it up with a wooden spoon
3. Then add in the onions, peppers, garlic and mushrooms, stir to combine, season with salt and pepper to taste. Sauté until the sausage crumbles have browned, stirring frequently for around 10 minutes
4. Add in the pepperoni and olives to the pan, sauté for 1-2 minutes.
5. Then add in the sauce, water, Italian seasoning, salt and pasta to the pan, stir to combine
6. Bring the pot to a boil

7. Once boiling, reduce the heat to medium low, cover and allow to simmer for 10 minutes, stirring occasionally
8. Remove the cover and continue to simmer for 3-5 minutes, stirring occasionally
9. Stir in 1/2 cup of shredded Mozzarella cheese, sprinkle the remaining cheese on top
10. Arrange a few more whole pepperonis on top of the cheese, broil for a few minutes until the cheese is bubbling and melted
11. Top with the parsley and Romano cheese
12. Allow to cool and distribute the pasta evenly among the containers. Store in the fridge for 3-4 days or in the freezer for 2 weeks.

To Serve: Reheat in the oven at 375 degrees for 1-2 minutes or until heated through.

Recipe Note: If you would like it to be spicy, you can also use hot Italian sausage.

Nutrition Facts Per Serving: Calories:450 | Total Fat: 21.9g| Total Carbs: 22g| Fiber: 5g| Protein: 43g

Quinoa Stuffed Eggplant with Tahini Sauce

Full of flavor and packed with veggies, you'll instantly fall in love with this Mediterranean quinoa stuffed eggplant recipe!

Prep Time: 5 Minutes

Cook Time: 30 Minutes

Total Time: 35 Minutes

Serves: 2

Ingredients:

- 1 eggplant
- 2 tbsp olive oil, divided
- 1 medium shallot, diced, about 1/2 cup
- 1 cup chopped button mushrooms, about 2 cups whole
- 5-6 Tuttorosso whole plum tomatoes, chopped
- 1 tbsp tomato juice from the can
- 1 tbsp chopped fresh parsley, plus more to garnish
- 2 garlic cloves, minced
- 1/2 cup cooked quinoa
- 1/2 tsp ground cumin
- Salt, to taste
- Pepper, to taste
- 1 tbsp tahini
- 1 tsp lemon juice
- 1/2 tsp garlic powder
- Water to thin

Directions:

1. Preheat the oven to 425 degrees F
2. Prepare the eggplant by cutting it in half lengthwise and scoop out some of the flesh
3. Place it on a baking sheet, drizzle with 1 tbsp of oil, sprinkle with salt
4. Bake for 20 minutes
5. In the meantime, add the remaining oil in a large skillet
6. Once heated, add the shallots and mushrooms, sauté until mushrooms have softened, about 5 minutes Add in the tomatoes, quinoa and spices, cook until the liquid has evaporated
7. Once the eggplant has cooked, reduce the oven temperature to 350 degrees F
8. Stuff each half with the tomato-quinoa mixture
9. Bake for another 10 minutes
10. Allow to cool completely

11. Distribute among the containers, store for 2 days

To Serve: Reheat in the microwave for 1-2 minutes or until heated through. Quickly whisk together tahini, lemon, garlic, water and a sprinkle of salt and pepper, drizzle tahini over eggplants and sprinkle with parsley and enjoy.

Nutritional Facts Per Serving: Calories:345 | Carbs: 38g| Total Fat: 19g | Protein: 9g

Greek Baked Cod

Prepared Greek style with spices, a mixture of lemon juice, olive oil and lots of garlic, this is one of the best cod recipes around! And it's ready in just 15 mins!

Prep Time: 10 Minutes

Cook Time: 12 Minutes

Total Time: 22 Minutes

Serves: 4

Ingredients:

- 1 ½ lb Cod fillet pieces (4–6 pieces)
- 5 garlic cloves, peeled and minced
- 1/4 cup chopped fresh parsley leaves

Lemon Juice Mixture:

- 5 tbsp fresh lemon juice
- 5 tbsp extra virgin olive oil
- 2 tbsp melted vegan butter

For Coating:

- 1/3 cup all-purpose flour
- 1 tsp ground coriander
- 3/4 tsp sweet Spanish paprika
- 3/4 tsp ground cumin
- 3/4 tsp salt
- 1/2 tsp black pepper

Directions:

1. Preheat oven to 400 degrees F
2. In a bowl, mix together lemon juice, olive oil, and melted butter, set aside
3. In another shallow bowl, mix all-purpose flour, spices, salt and pepper, set next to the lemon bowl to create a station
4. Pat the fish fillet dry, then dip the fish in the lemon juice mixture then dip it in the flour mixture, shake off excess flour
5. In a cast iron skillet over medium-high heat, add 2 tbsp olive oil
6. Once heated, add in the fish and sear on each side for color, but do not fully cook (just couple minutes on each side), remove from heat
7. With the remaining lemon juice mixture, add the minced garlic and mix
8. Drizzle all over the fish fillets
9. Bake for 10 minutes, for until the it begins to flake easily with a fork
10. allow the dish to cool completely
11. Distribute among the containers, store for 2-3 days

To Serve: Reheat in the microwave for 1-2 minutes or until heated through. Sprinkle chopped parsley. Enjoy!

Nutritional Facts Per Serving: Calories:321 | Carbs: 16g| Total Fat: 18g | Protein: 23g

Lasagna Tortellini Soup

Easy crockpot lasagna soup? Yes please! It's made with cheese-filled tortellini in a delicious tomato sauce.

Prep Time: 15 Minutes
Cook Time: 6 Hours
Total Time: 6 Hours 15 Minutes
Serves: 6

Ingredients:

- 1 lb extra lean ground beef
- 1 package (16 oz) frozen cheese filled tortellini
- 3 cups beef broth
- 1/2 cup yellow onion, chopped
- 2 cloves garlic, minced
- 1 can (28 oz) crushed tomatoes
- 1 can (14.5 oz) petite diced tomatoes
- 1 can (6 oz) tomato paste
- 1 can (10.75 oz) tomato condensed soup
- 1 tsp white sugar
- 1 ½ tsp dried basil
- 1 tsp Italian seasoning
- 1/2 tbsp salt, to taste
- 1/4 tsp pepper

Optional:

- 4 tbsp fresh parsley
- 1/2 tsp fennel seeds

Toppings:

- Freshly grated Parmesan cheese
- Large spoonful of ricotta cheese

Directions:

1. In a large skillet over medium heat, brown the ground beef until cooked through
2. Add the onion and garlic in the last few minutes of the cooking
3. While the beef is cooking, pour in the crushed tomatoes, petite diced tomatoes, tomato paste, and tomato condensed soup in the slow cooker. - Don't drain the cans!
4. Add in the sugar, the dried basil, fennel, Italian seasoning, salt, and pepper, adjust to taste
5. Stir in the cooked ground beef with onions and garlic

6. Add in the beef broth – or dissolved beef bouillon cubes into boiling water
7. Cook on high for 3-4 hours or low for 5-7 hours.
8. 15-20 minutes before you are ready to serve the soup, add in the frozen tortellini
9. Set the slow cooker to high and allow the tortellini to heat through
10. Allow to cool, then distribute the soup into the container and store in the fridge for up to 3 days

To Serve: Reheat in the microwave or on the stove top, top with freshly grated Parmesan cheese, a large spoonful of ricotta cheese, extra seasonings and freshly chopped parsley.

Nutrition Facts Per Serving: Calories:499 | Total Fat: 17g| Total Carbs: 53g| Fiber: 8g| Protein: 34g

Greek Quinoa Bowls

Loaded with fresh veggies, these tasty Greek Quinoa Bowls are easy to make and of course, so delicious!

Prep Time: 3 Minutes

Cook Time: 12 Minutes

Total Time: 15 Minutes

Serves: 2

Ingredients:

- 1 cup quinoa
- 1 ½ cups water
- 1 cup chopped green bell pepper
- 1 cup chopped red bell pepper
- 1/3 cup crumbled feta cheese
- 1/4 cup extra virgin olive oil
- 2-3 tbsp apple cider vinegar
- Salt, to taste
- Pepper, to taste
- 1-2 tbsp fresh parsley

To Serve:

- Hummus
- Pita wedges
- Olives
- Fresh tomatoes
- Sliced or chopped avocado
- Lemon wedges

Directions:

1. Rinse and drain the quinoa using a mesh strainer or sieve. Place a medium saucepan to medium heat and lightly toast the quinoa to remove any excess water. Stir as it toasts for just a few minutes, to add a nuttiness and fluff to the quinoa
2. Then add the water, set burner to high, and bring to a boil.
3. Once boiling, reduce heat to low and simmer, covered with the lid slightly ajar, for 12-13 minutes or until quinoa is fluffy and the liquid have been absorbed
4. In the meantime, mix whisk together olive oil, apple cider vinegar, salt, and pepper to make the dressing, store in the fridge until ready to serve
5. Add in the red bell peppers, green bell peppers, and parsley
6. Give the quinoa a little fluff with a fork, remove from the pot
7. Allow to cool completely

8. Distribute among the containers, store for 2-3 days

To Serve: Reheat in the microwave for 1-2 minutes or until heated through. Pour the dressing over the quinoa bowl, toss add the feta cheese. Season with additional salt and pepper to taste, if desired. Enjoy!

Nutritional Facts Per Serving: Calories:645 | Carbs: 61g| Total Fat: 37g | Protein: 16g

Baked Shrimp Stew

This hearty shrimp stew recipe is flavor-packed and swimming in a Eastern Mediterranean chunky tomato sauce.

Prep Time: 20 Minutes
Cook Time: 25 Minutes
Total Time: 45 Minutes
Serves: 4-6

Ingredients:

- Greek extra virgin olive oil
- 2 1/2 lb prawns, peeled, deveined, rinsed well and dried
- 1 large red onion, chopped (about two cups)
- 5 garlic cloves, roughly chopped
- 1 red bell pepper, seeded, chopped
- 2 15-oz cans diced tomatoes
- 1/2 cup water
- 1 1/2 tsp ground coriander
- 1 tsp sumac
- 1 tsp cumin
- 1 tsp red pepper flakes, more to taste
- 1/2 tsp ground green cardamom
- Salt and pepper, to taste
- 1 cup parsley leaves, stems removed
- 1/3 cup toasted pine nuts
- 1/4 cup toasted sesame seeds
- Lemon or lime wedges to serve

Directions:

1. Preheat the oven to 375 degrees F
2. In a large frying pan, add 1 tbsp olive oil
3. Sauté the prawns for 2 minutes, until they are barely pink, then remove and set aside
4. In the same pan over medium-high heat, drizzle a little more olive oil and sauté the chopped onions, garlic and red bell peppers for 4-5 minutes, stirring regularly
5. Add in the canned diced tomatoes and water, allow to simmer for 10 minutes, until the liquid reduces, stir occasionally
6. Reduce the heat to medium, add the shrimp back to the pan, stir in the spices the ground coriander, sumac, cumin, red pepper flakes, green cardamom, salt and

pepper, then the toasted pine nuts, sesame seeds and parsley leaves, stir to combined

7. Transfer the shrimp and sauce to an oven-safe earthenware or stoneware dish, cover tightly with foil Place in the oven to bake for 7 minutes, uncover and broil briefly.

8. allow the dish to cool completely

9. Distribute among the containers, store for 2-3 days

To Serve: Reheat on the stove for 1-2 minutes or until heated through. Serve with your favorite bread or whole grain. Garnish with a side of lime or lemon wedges.

Nutritional Facts Per Serving: Calories:377 | Carbs: 11g| Total Fat: 20g | Protein: 41g

Baked Tilapia

Seasoned with Mediterranean spices and herbs, this recipe for baked tilapia is moist, flaky and perfect for dinner! Serve it up with your favorite grain and roasted veggies.

Prep Time: 10 Minutes

Cook Time: 15 Minutes

Total Time: 25 Minutes

Serves: 4

Ingredients:

- 1 lb tilapia fillets (about 8 fillets)
- 1 tsp olive oil
- 1 tbsp vegan butter
- 2 shallots finely chopped
- 3 garlic cloves minced
- 1 1/2 tsp ground cumin
- 1 1/2 tsp paprika
- 1/4 cup capers
- 1/4 cup fresh dill finely chopped
- Juice from 1 lemon
- Salt & Pepper to taste

Directions:

1. Preheat oven to 375 degrees F
2. Line a rimmed baking sheet with parchment paper or foil
3. Lightly mist with cooking spray, arrange the fish fillets evenly on baking sheet
4. In a small bowl, combine the cumin, paprika, salt and pepper
5. Season both sides of the fish fillets with the spice mixture
6. In a small bowl, whisk together the melted butter, lemon juice, shallots, olive oil, and garlic, and brush evenly over fish fillets
7. Top with the capers
8. Bake in the oven for 10-15 minutes, until cook through, but not overcooked
9. Remove from oven and allow the dish to cool completely
10. Distribute among the containers, store for 2-3 days

To Serve: Reheat in the microwave for 1-2 minutes or until heated through. Top with fresh dill. Serve!

Nutritional Facts Per Serving: Calories:129 | Total Fat: 5g | Protein: 21g

One Skillet Chicken in Roasted Red Pepper Sauce

Roasted red peppers and chicken come together in this easy one skillet meal that you can enjoy with your favorite whole grains and fresh veggies!

Prep Time: 5 Minutes

Cook Time: 20 Minutes

Total Time: 25 Minutes

Serves: 4

Ingredients:

- 4-6 boneless skinless chicken thighs or breasts
- 2/3 cup chopped roasted red peppers (see note)
- 2 tsp Italian seasoning, divided
- 4 tbsp oil
- 1 tbsp minced garlic
- 1/2 tsp salt
- 1/4 tsp black pepper
- 1 cup heavy cream
- 2 tbsp crumbled feta cheese, optional
- Thinly sliced fresh basil, optional

Directions:

1. In a blender or food processer, combine the roasted red peppers, 1 tsp Italian seasoning, oil, garlic, salt, and pepper, pulse until smooth.
2. In a large skillet over medium heat, add the olive oil and season chicken with remaining 1 tsp Italian seasoning. Cook chicken for 6-8 minutes on each side, or until cooked through and lightly browned on the outside. Then transfer to a plate and cover
3. Add the red pepper mixture to the pan, stir over medium heat 2-3 minutes, or until heated throughout. Add the heavy cream, stir until mixture is thick and creamy
4. Add chicken, toss in the sauce to coat
5. allow the dish to cool completely
6. Distribute among the containers, store for 2-3 days

To Serve: Reheat in the microwave for 1-2 minutes or until heated through. Garnish with crumbled feta cheese and fresh basil. Serve with your favorite grain.

Recipe Notes: You can purchase jarred roasted red peppers at most grocery stores around the olives.

Nutritional Facts Per Serving: Calories:655 | Carbs: 12g| Total Fat: 25g | Protein: 89g

Skillet Shrimp with Summer Squash and Chorizo

Seasoned to perfection, this shrimp and Chorizo recipe has an unforgettable South-of-Spain twist!

Prep Time: 10 Minutes
Cook Time: 20 Minutes
Total Time: 30 Minutes
Serves: 8

Ingredients:

- 1 lb large shrimp or prawns, peeled and deveined, tail can remain or frozen frozen, thawed
- 7 oz Spanish Chorizo, or mild Chorizo or hot Chorizo, sliced
- Extra virgin olive oil
- Juice of 1/2 lemon
- 1 summer squash, halved then sliced, half moons
- 1 small hot pepper such as jalapeno pepper, optional
- 1/2 medium red onion, sliced
- Fresh parsley for garnish
- 3/4 tsp smoked paprika
- 3/4 tsp ground cumin
- 1/2 tsp garlic powder
- Salt, to taste
- Pepper, to taste

Directions:

1. Pat shrimp dry, then season with salt, pepper, paprika, cumin, and garlic powder, toss to coat, set aside
2. In a large cast iron skillet over medium-high, add the Chorizo and brown on both sides, about 4 minutes or until the Chorizo is cooked, transfer to a plate
3. In the same skillet, add a drizzle of extra virgin olive oil if needed
4. Add the summer squash, and a sprinkle of salt and pepper and sear undisturbed for about 3 to 4 minutes on one side. turnover and sear another 2 minutes on the other side until nicely colored, transfer the squash to the plate with Chorizo
5. In the same skillet, now add a little extra virgin olive oil and tilting to make sure the bottom is well coated
6. Once heated, add the shrimp and cook, stirring frequently, until the shrimp flesh starts to turn a little pink, but still not quite fully cooked, about 3 minutes
7. Return the Chorizo and squash to the skillet, toss to combine, cook another 3 minutes or until shrimp is cooked – its pink and the tails turn a bright red

8. Transfer the shrimp skillet to a large serving platter, allow to cool
9. Distribute among the containers, store for 2-3 days

To Serve: Reheat on the stove for 1-2 minutes or until heated through. Squeeze 1/2 lemon on top, and sliced red onions and hot peppers.

Nutritional Facts Per Serving: Calories:192 | Carbs: 4g| Total Fat: 11g | Protein: 17g

Steak and Veggies

Dig into a melt-in-your-mouth tender steak with potatoes and broccoli that's all cook on one baking sheet.

Prep Time: 15 Minutes

Cook Time: 15 Minutes

Total Time: 30 Minutes

Serves: 6

Ingredients:

- 2 lbs baby red potatoes
- 16 oz broccoli florets
- 2 tbsp olive oil
- 3 cloves garlic, minced
- 1 tsp dried thyme
- Kosher salt, to taste
- Freshly ground black pepper, to taste
- 2 lbs (1-inch-thick) top sirloin steak, patted dry

Directions:

1. Preheat oven to broil
2. Lightly oil a baking sheet or coat with nonstick spray
3. In a large pot over high heat, boil salted water, cook the potatoes until parboiled for 12-15 minutes, drain well
4. Place the potatoes and broccoli in a single layer onto the prepared baking sheet
5. Add the olive oil, garlic and thyme, season with salt and pepper, to taste and then gently toss to combine
6. Season the steaks with salt and pepper, to taste, and add to the baking sheet in a single layer
7. Place it into oven and broil until the steak is browned and charred at the edges, about 4-5 minutes per side for medium-rare, or until the desired doneness
8. Distribute the steak and veggies among the containers. Store in the fridge for up to 3 days

To Serve: Reheat in the microwave for 1-2 minutes. Top with garlic butter and enjoy

Nutrition Facts Per Serving: Calories:460 | Total Fat: 24g| Total Carbs: 24g| Fiber: 2.6g| Protein: 37g

Greek Lemon Chicken Soup

This Greek Lemon Chicken Soup Recipe is light, healthy and full of bold Greek flavors!

Prep Time: 10 Minutes

Cook Time: 20 Minutes

Total Time: 30 Minutes

Serves: 8

Ingredients:

- 10 cups chicken broth
- 3 tbsp olive oil
- 8 cloves garlic, minced
- 1 sweet onion
- 1 large lemon, zested
- 2 boneless skinless chicken breasts
- 1 cup Israeli couscous (pearl)
- 1/2 tsp crushed red pepper
- 2 oz crumbled feta
- 1/3 cup chopped chive
- Salt, to taste
- Pepper, to taste

Directions:

1. In a large 6-8-quart sauce pot over medium-low heat, add the olive oil
2. Once heated, sauté the onion and minced the garlic for 3-4 minutes to soften
3. Then add in the chicken broth, raw chicken breasts, lemon zest, and crushed red pepper to the pot Raise the heat to high, cover, and bring to a boil
4. Once boiling, reduce the heat to medium, then simmer for 5 minutes
5. Stir in the couscous, 1 tsp salt, and black pepper to taste
6. Simmer another 5 minute, then turn the heat off
7. Using tongs, remove the two chicken breasts from the pot and transfer to a plate
8. Use a fork and the tongs to shred the chicken, then return to the pot
9. Stir in the crumbled feta cheese and chopped chive
10. Season to taste with salt and pepper as needed
11. Allow the soup to cool completely
12. Distribute among the containers, store for 2-3 days

To Serve: Reheat in the microwave for 1-2 minutes or until heated through, or reheat on the stove

Nutritional Facts Per Serving: Calories:214 | Carbs: 23g| Total Fat: g | Protein: 11g

Greek Turkey Meatball Gyro with Tzatziki

These 30 Minute Greek Turkey Meatball Gyros are so juicy, moist and topped with a classic Tzatziki Sauce!

Prep Time: 10 Minutes
Cook Time: 16 Minutes
Total Time: 26 Minutes
Serves: 4

Ingredients:

Turkey Meatball:

- 1 lb. ground turkey
- 1/4 cup finely diced red onion
- 2 garlic cloves, minced
- 1 tsp oregano
- 1 cup chopped fresh spinach
- Salt, to taste
- Pepper, to taste
- 2 tbsp olive oil

Tzatziki Sauce:

- 1/2 cup plain Greek yogurt
- 1/4 cup grated cucumber
- 2 tbsp lemon juice
- 1/2 tsp dry dill
- 1/2 tsp garlic powder
- Salt, to taste
- 1/2 cup thinly sliced red onion
- 1 cup diced tomato
- 1 cup diced cucumber
- 4 whole wheat flatbreads

Directions:

1. In a large bowl, add in ground turkey, diced red onion, oregano, fresh spinach minced garlic, salt, and pepper
2. Using your hands mix all the ingredients together until the meat forms a ball and sticks together
3. Then using your hands, form meat mixture into 1″ balls, making about 12 meatballs
4. In a large skillet over medium high heat, add the olive oil and then add the meatballs, cook each side for 3-4 minutes until they are browned on all sides, remove from the pan and allow it to rest

5. Allow the dish to cool completely
6. Distribute in the container, store for 2-3 days

To Serve: Reheat in the microwave for 1-2 minutes or until heated through. In the meantime, in a small bowl, combine the Greek yogurt, grated cucumber, lemon juice, dill, garlic powder, and salt to taste Assemble the gyros by taking the toasted flatbread, add 3 meatballs, sliced red onion, tomato, and cucumber. Top with Tzatziki sauce and serve!

Nutritional Facts Per Serving: Calories:429 | Carbs: 38g| Total Fat: 19g | Protein: 28g

Pesto Chicken and Tomato Zoodles

Full of bold flavors, high in protein, and in low carbs, everyone will love this Pesto Chicken and Tomato Zoodle dish!

Prep Time: 5 Minutes

Cook Time: 15 Minutes

Total Time: 20 Minutes

Serves: 4

Ingredients:

- 3 Zucchini, inspiralized
- 2 boneless skinless chicken breasts
- 1 1/2 cup cherry tomatoes
- 2 tsp olive oil
- 1/2 tsp salt
- Store brought Pesto or Homemade Basil Pesto
- Salt, to taste
- Pepper, to taste

Directions:

1. Preheat grill to medium high heat
2. Season both sides of the chicken with salt and pepper
3. Place cherry tomatoes in a small bowl, add the olive oil and 1/2 tsp salt, and toss the tomatoes
4. In the meantime, inspiralize the zucchini, set aside
5. Pour the pesto over the zucchini noodles, using salad toss or tongs, mix the pesto in with the zoodles until it is completely combined
6. Place the chicken on the grill and grill each side for 5-7 minutes, or until cooked through
7. Place cherry tomatoes in a grill basket and grill for 5 minutes, until tomatoes burst
8. Remove the tomatoes and chicken from the grill, slice the chicken and place both sliced chicken and tomatoes into the pesto zoodles bowl
9. allow the dish to cool completely
10. Distribute among the containers, store for 2-3 days

To Serve: Reheat in the microwave for 1-2 minutes or until heated through. Enjoy

Nutritional Facts Per Serving: Calories:396 | Carbs: 8g| Total Fat: 30g | Protein: 18g

Greek Shrimp and Farro Bowls

Hearty and ready in just 30 minutes, this dish features zesty lemon and herb shrimp with bell peppers, zucchini, tomatoes, and olives on a bed of toasty, whole-grain farro.

Prep Time: 10 Minutes

Cook Time: 20 Minutes

Total Time: 30 Minutes

Serves: 4

Ingredients:

- 1 lb peeled and deveined shrimp
- 3 Tbsp. extra virgin olive oil
- 2 cloves garlic, minced
- 2 bell peppers, sliced thick
- 2 medium-sized zucchinis, sliced into thin rounds
- pint cherry tomatoes, halved
- ¼ cup thinly sliced green or black olives
- 4 Tbsp. 2% reduced-fat plain Greek yogurt
- Juice of 1 lemon
- 2 tsp fresh chopped dill
- 1 Tbsp. fresh chopped oregano
- ½ tsp smoked paprika
- ½ tsp sea salt
- ¼ tsp black pepper
- 1 cup dry farro

Directions:

1. In a bowl, add the olive oil, garlic, lemon, dill, oregano, paprika, salt, and pepper, whisk to combine
2. Pour 3/4 the amount of marinade over shrimp, toss to coat and all to stand 10 minutes
3. Reserve the rest of the marinade for later
4. Cook the farro according to package instructions in water or chicken stock
5. In a grill pan or nonstick skillet over medium heat, add the olive
6. Once heated, add shrimp, cook for 2-3 minutes per side, until no longer pink, then transfer to a plate
7. Working in batches, cook bell pepper, zucchinis, and cherry tomatoes to the grill pan or skillet, cook for 5-6 minutes, until softened
8. allow the dish to cool completely

9. Distribute the farro among the containers, evenly add the shrimp, grilled vegetables, olives, and tomatoes, store for 2 days

To Serve: Reheat in the microwave for 1-2 minutes or until heated through. Drizzle the reserved marinade over top. Top each bowl with 1 tbsp Greek yogurt and extra lemon juice, if desired

Nutritional Facts Per Serving: Calories:428 | Carbs: 45g| Total Fat: 13g | Protein: 34g

Zesty Lemon Parmesan Chicken and Zucchini Noodles

Perfect for any day of the week, this Lemon Parmesan Chicken with Zucchini Noodles will come together quickly and is packed with flavor!

Prep Time: 5 Minutes
Cook Time: 15 Minutes
Total Time: 20 Minutes
Serves: 2

Ingredients:

- 2 packages Frozen zucchini noodle Spirals
- 1-1/2 lbs. boneless skinless chicken breast, cut into bite-sized pieces
- 1 tsp fine sea salt
- 2 tsp dried oregano
- 1/2 tsp ground black pepper
- 4 garlic cloves, minced
- 2 tbsp vegan butter
- 2 tsp lemon zest
- 2 tsp oil
- 1/3 cup parmesan
- 2/3 cup broth
- Lemon slices, for garnish
- Parsley, for garnish

Directions:

1. Cook zucchini noodles according to package instructions, drain well
2. In a large skillet over medium heat, add the oil
3. Season chicken with salt and pepper, brown chicken pieces, for about 3-4 minutes per side depending on the thickness, or until cooked through – Work in cook in batches if necessary
4. Transfer the chicken to a pan
5. In the same skillet, add in the garlic, and cook until fragrant about 30 seconds
6. Add in the butter, oregano and lemon zest, pour in chicken broth to deglaze making sure to scrape up all the browned bits stuck to the bottom of the pan
7. Turn the heat up to medium-high, bring sauce and chicken up to a boil, immediately lower the heat and stir in the parmesan cheese
8. Place the chicken back in pan and allow it to gently simmer for 3-4 minutes, or until sauce has slightly reduced and thickened up
9. Taste and adjust seasoning, allow the noodles to cool completely
10. Distribute among the containers, store for 2-3 days

To Serve: Reheat in the microwave for 1-2 minutes or until heated through. Garnish with the fresh parsley and lemon slices and enjoy!

Nutritional Facts Per Serving: Calories:633 | Carbs: 4g| Total Fat: 35g | Protein: 70g

Mediterranean Pearl Couscous

Made with Mediterranean staples–chickpeas, artichoke hearts, and pearl couscous, this fresh salad makes for a light and delicious lunch or dinner.

Prep Time: 15 Minutes

Cook Time: 10 Minutes

Total Time: 25 Minutes

Serves: 6

Ingredients:

For the Lemon Dill Vinaigrette:

- 1 large lemon, juice of
- 1/3 cup Extra virgin olive oil
- 1 tsp dill weed
- 1 tsp garlic powder
- Salt and pepper

For the Israeli Couscous:

- 2 cups Pearl Couscous, Israeli Couscous
- Extra virgin olive oil
- 2 cups grape tomatoes, halved
- 1/3 cup finely chopped red onions
- 1/2 English cucumber, finely chopped
- 15 oz can chickpeas
- 14 oz can good quality artichoke hearts, roughly chopped if needed
- 1/2 cup good pitted kalamata olives
- 15–20 fresh basil leaves, roughly chopped or torn; more for garnish
- 3 oz fresh baby mozzarella or feta cheese, optional
- Water

Directions:

1. Make the lemon-dill vinaigrette, place the lemon juice, olive oil, dill weed, garlic powder, salt and pepper in a bowl, whisk together to combine and set aside
2. In a medium-sized heavy pot, heat two tbsp of olive oil
3. Sauté the couscous in the olive oil briefly until golden brown, then add 3 cups of boiling water (or follow the instructed on the package), and cook according to package.
4. Once done, drain in a colander, set aside in a bowl and allow to cool
5. In a large mixing bowl, combine the extra virgin olive oil, grape tomatoes, red onions, cucumber, chickpeas, artichoke hearts, and kalamata olives
6. Then add in the couscous and the basil, mix together gently

7. Now, give the lemon-dill vinaigrette a quick whisk and add to the couscous salad, mix to combine
8. Taste and adjust salt, if needed
9. Distribute among the containers, store for 2-3 days

To Serve: Add in the mozzarella cheese, garnish with more fresh basil and enjoy!

Nutritional Facts Per Serving: Calories:393 | Carbs: 57g| Total Fat: 13g | Protein: 13g

Steak Cobb Salad

A juicy steak, spinach, tomatoes, eggs and feta, come together to make this amazing dish!

Prep Time: 30 Minutes
Cook Time: 15 Minutes
Total Time: 45 Minutes
Serves: 4

Ingredients:

- 6 large eggs
- 2 tbsp unsalted butter
- 1 lb steak
- 2 tbsp olive oil
- 6 cups baby spinach
- 1 cup cherry tomatoes, halved
- 1 cup pecan halves
- 1/2 cup crumbled feta cheese
- Kosher salt, to taste
- Freshly ground black pepper, to taste

Directions:

1. In a large skillet over medium high heat, melt butter
2. Using paper towels, pat the steak dry, then drizzle with olive oil and season with salt and pepper, to taste
3. Once heated, add the steak to the skillet and cook, flipping once, until cooked through to desired doneness, - cook for 3-4 minutes per side for a medium-rare steak
4. Transfer the steak to a plate and allow it to cool before dicing
5. Place the eggs in a large saucepan and cover with cold water by 1 inch
6. Bring to a boil and cook for 1 minute, cover the eggs with a tight-fitting lid and remove from heat, set aside for 8-10 minutes, then drain well and allow to cool before peeling and dicing
7. Assemble the salad in the container by placing the spinach at the bottom of the container, top with arranged rows of steak, eggs, feta, tomatoes, and pecans

To Serve: Top with the balsamic vinaigrette, or desired dressing

Recipe Note: You can also use New York, rib-eye or filet mignon for this recipe

Nutrition Facts Per Serving: Calories:640 | Total Fat: 51g| Total Carbs: 9.8g| Fiber: 5g| Protein: 38.8g

Grilled Mediterranean Chicken Kebabs

Serve up these delicious and easy grilled Mediterranean Chicken Kebabs with a fresh salad or your favorite grilled vegetables!

Prep Time: 40 Minutes
Cook Time: 10 Minutes
Total Time: 55 Minutes
Serves: 10 Skewers

Ingredients:

Chicken Kebabs:

- 3 chicken fillets, cut in 1-inch cubes
- 2 red bell peppers
- 2 green bell peppers
- 1 red onion

Chicken Kebab Marinade:

- 2/3 cup extra virgin olive oil, divided
- Juice of 1 lemon, divided
- 6 clove of garlic, chopped, divided
- 4 tsp salt, divided
- 2 tsp freshly ground black pepper, divided
- 2 tsp paprika, divided
- 2 tsp thyme, divided
- 4 tsp oregano, divided

Directions:

- In a bowl, mix 1/2 of all ingredients for the marinade- olive oils, lemon juice, garlic, salt, pepper, paprika, thyme and oregano in small bowl
- Place the chicken in a ziplock bag and pour marinade over it, marinade in the fridge for about 30 minutes
- In a separate ziplock bag, mix the other half of the marinade ingredients - olive oils, lemon juice, garlic, salt, pepper, paprika, thyme and oregano - add the vegetables and marinade for at least 30 minutes
- If you are using wood skewers, soak the skewers in water for about 20-30 minutes
- Once done, thread the chicken and peppers and onions on the skewers in a pattern about 5-6 pieces of chicken with peppers and onion in between
- Over an outdoor grill or indoor grill pan over medium-high heat, spray the grates lightly with oil
- Grill the chicken for about 5 minutes on each side, or until cooked through, then allow to cool completely

- Distribute among the containers, store for 2-3 days

To Serve: Reheat in the microwave for 1-2 minutes or until heated through, or cover in foil and reheat in the oven at 375 degrees F for 5 minutes

Recipe Notes: You can also bake the Mediterranean chicken skewers in the oven. Just preheat the oven to 425 F and place the chicken skewers on roasting racks that are over two foil-lined baking sheets. Bake for 10-15 minutes, turn over and bake for an additional 10 - 15 minutes on the other side, or until cooked through

Nutritional Facts Per Serving: Calories:228 | Carbs: 5g| Total Fat: 17g | Protein: 14g

Mediterranean Baked Sole Fillet

Spiced Mediterranean-style and baked in a buttery lime sauce, this baked sole dish is simple and delicious!

Prep Time: 15 Minutes

Cook Time: 15 Minutes

Total Time: 30 Minutes

Serves: 6

Ingredients:

- 1 lime or lemon, juice of
- 1/2 cup extra virgin olive oil
- 3 tbsp unsalted melted vegan butter
- 2 shallots, thinly sliced
- 3 garlic cloves, thinly-sliced
- 2 tbsp capers
- 1.5 lb Sole fillet, about 10–12 thin fillets
- 4–6 green onions, top trimmed, halved lengthwise
- 1 lime or lemon, sliced (optional)
- 3/4 cup roughly chopped fresh dill for garnish
- 1 tsp seasoned salt, or to your taste
- 3/4 tsp ground black pepper
- 1 tsp ground cumin
- 1 tsp garlic powder

Directions:

1. Preheat over to 375-degree F
2. In a small bowl, whisk together olive oil, lime juice, and melted butter with a sprinkle of seasoned salt, stir in the garlic, shallots, and capers.
3. In a separate small bowl, mix together the pepper, cumin, seasoned salt, and garlic powder, season the fish fillets each on both sides
4. On a large baking pan or dish, arrange the fish fillets and cover with the buttery lime
5. Arrange the green onion halves and lime slices on top
6. Bake in 375 degrees F for 10-15 minutes, do not overcook
7. Remove the fish fillets from the oven
8. Allow the dish to cool completely
9. Distribute among the containers, store for 2-3 days

To Serve: Reheat in the microwave for 1-2 minutes or until heated through. Garnish with the chopped fresh dill. Serve with your favorite and a fresh salad

Recipe Notes: If you can't get your hands on a sole fillet, cook this recipe with a different white fish. Just remember to change the baking time since it will be different.

Nutritional Facts Per Serving: Calories:350 | Carbs:7 g| Total Fat: 26g | Protein: 23g

Italian Skillet Chicken with Mushrooms and Tomatoes

A flavor-packed skillet chicken dinner with a twist! These chicken cutlets are cooked in a white wine sauce with garlic, tomatoes, and mushrooms!

Prep Time: 10 Minutes

Cook Time: 20 Minutes

Total Time: 30 Minutes

Serves: 4

Ingredients:

- 4 large chicken cutlets, boneless skinless chicken breasts cut into 1/4-inch thin cutlets
- 1 tbsp dried oregano, divided
- 1/2 cup all-purpose flour, more for later
- 8 oz Baby Bella mushrooms, cleaned, trimmed, and sliced
- 14 oz grape tomatoes, halved
- 2 tbsp chopped fresh garlic
- Extra Virgin Olive Oil
- 1/2 cup white wine
- 1 tbsp freshly squeezed lemon juice, juice of 1/2 lemon
- 1 tsp salt, divided
- 1 tsp black pepper, divided
- 3/4 cup chicken broth
- Handful baby spinach, optional

Directions:

1. Pat the chicken cutlets dry, season both sides with 1/2 tsp salt, 1/2 tsp black pepper, 1/2 tbsp dried oregano,
2. Coat the chicken cutlets with the flour, gently dust-off excess and set aside
3. In a large cast iron skillet with a lid, heat 2 tbsp olive oil
4. Once heated, brown the chicken cutlets on both sides, for about 3 minutes, then transfer the chicken cutlets to plate
5. In the same skillet, add more olive oil if needed,
6. Once heated, add in the mushrooms and sauté on medium-high for about 1 minute
7. Then add the tomatoes, garlic, the remaining 1/2 tbsp oregano, 1/2 tsp salt, and 1/2 tsp pepper, and 2 tsp flour, cook for 3 minutes or so, stirring regularly
8. Add in the white wine, cook briefly to reduce, then add the lemon juice and chicken broth

9. Bring the liquid to a boil, then transfer the chicken back into the skillet, cook over high heat for 3-4 minutes, then reduce the heat to medium-low, cover and cook for another 8 minutes or until the chicken is cooked through
10. Allow the dish to cool completely
11. Distribute among the containers, store for 3 days

To Serve: Reheat in the microwave for 1-2 minutes or until heated through. Serve with baby spinach, your favorite small pasta and a crusty Italian bread!

Nutritional Facts Per Serving: Calories:218 | Carbs: 16g| Total Fat: 6g | Protein: 23g

Greek Chicken Wraps

Now, these Greek chicken wraps are perfect for lunch or dinner! Ready in just 30 minutes, they're filled with seasoned chicken, fresh vegetables, and Greek flavors!

Prep Time: 14 minutes
Cook Time: 15 minutes
Total Time: 29 minutes
Serves: 2

Ingredients:

Greek Chicken Wrap Filling:

- 2 chicken breasts 14 oz, chopped into 1-inch pieces
- 2 small zucchinis, cut into 1-inch pieces
- 2 bell peppers, cut into 1-inch pieces
- 1 red onion, cut into 1-inch pieces
- 2 tbsp olive oil
- 2 tsp oregano
- 2 tsp basil
- 1/2 tsp garlic powder
- 1/2 tsp onion powder
- 1/2 tsp salt
- 2 lemons, sliced

To Serve:

- 1/4 cup feta cheese crumbled
- 4 large flour tortillas or wraps

Directions:

1. Pre-heat oven to 425 degrees F
2. In a bowl, toss together the chicken, zucchinis, olive oil, oregano, basil, garlic, bell peppers, onion powder, onion powder and salt
3. Arrange lemon slice on the baking sheet(s), spread the chicken and vegetable out on top (use 2 baking sheets if needed)
4. Bake for 15 minutes, until veggies are soft and the chicken is cooked through
5. Allow to cool completely
6. Distribute the chicken, bell pepper, zucchini and onions among the containers and remove the lemon slices
7. Allow the dish to cool completely
8. Distribute among the containers, store for 3 days

To Serve: Reheat in the microwave for 1-2 minutes or until heated through. Wrap in a tortila and sprinkle with feta cheese. Enjoy!

Nutrition Facts Per Serving (1 wrap): Calories:356 | Total Fat: 14g| Total Carbs: 26g| Protein: 29g

Zoodles with Turkey Meatballs

Skip the classic spaghetti and make this heathier version made with yummy zoodles and juicy turkey meatballs!

Prep Time: 1 Hour
Cook Time: 30 Minutes
Total Time: 1 Hour 30 Minutes
Serves: 4-6

Ingredients:

- 2 lbs (3 medium-sized) zucchini, spiralized
- 2 cups marinara sauce, store-bought
- 1/4 cup freshly grated Parmesan cheese
- 2 tsp salt

For The Meatballs:

- 1 ½ lbs ground turkey
- 1/2 cup Panko
- 1/4 cup freshly grated Parmesan cheese
- 2 large egg yolks
- 1 tsp dried oregano
- 1 tsp dried basil
- 1/2 tsp dried parsley
- 1/4 tsp garlic powder
- 1/4 tsp crushed red pepper flakes
- Kosher salt, to taste
- Freshly ground black pepper, to taste

Directions:

1. Preheat oven to 400 degrees F
2. Lightly oil a 9×13 baking dish or spray with nonstick spray
3. In a large bowl, combine the ground turkey, egg yolks, oregano, basil, Panko, Parmesan, parsley, garlic powder and red pepper flakes, season the mixture with salt and pepper, to taste
4. Use a wooden spoon or clean hands, stir well to combined
5. Roll the mixture into 1 1/2-to-2-inch meatballs, forming about 24 meatballs
6. Place the meatballs onto the prepared baking dish
7. Bake for 18-20 minutes, or until browned and the meatballs are cooked through, set aside
8. Place the zucchini in a colander over the sink, add the salt and gently toss to combine, allow to sit for 10 minutes

9. In a large pot of boiling water, cook zucchini for 30 seconds to 1 minute, drain well
10. Allow to cool, then distribute the zucchini into the containers, top with the meatballs, marinara sauce and the Parmesan. Store in the fridge for up to 4 days

To Serve: Reheat in the microwave for 1-2 minutes or until heated through and enjoy!

Nutrition Facts Per Serving: Calories:279 | Total Fat: 13g| Total Carbs: 12g| Fiber: 3g| Protein: 31g

Rainbow Salad with Roasted Chickpeas

This vibrant rainbow salad is made with zucchini, colorful carrots, fresh basil, and spiced roasted chickpeas!

Prep Time: 15 Minutes
Cook Time: 40 Minutes
Total Time: 55 Minutes
Serves: 2-3

Ingredients:

- Creamy avocado dressing, store bought or homemade
- 3 large tri-color carrots - one orange, one red, and one yellow
- 1 medium zucchini
- 1/4 cup fresh basil, cut into ribbons
- 1 can chickpeas, rinsed and drained
- 1 tbsp olive oil
- 1 tsp chili powder
- 1/2 tsp cumin
- Salt, to taste
- Pepper, to taste

Directions:

1. Preheat the oven to 400 degrees F
2. Pat the chickpeas dry with paper towels
3. Add them to a bowl and toss with the olive oil, chili powder, cumin, and salt and pepper
4. Arrange the chickpeas on a baking sheet in a single layer
5. Bake for 30-40 minutes - making sure to shaking the pan once in a while to prevent over browning. The chickpeas will be done when they're crispy and golden brown, allow to cool
6. With a grater, peeler, mandolin or spiralizer, shred the carrots and zucchini into very thin ribbons
7. Once the zucchini is shredded, lightly press it with paper towels to remove excess moisture
8. Add the shredded zucchini and carrots to a bowl, toss with the basil
9. Add in the roasted chickpeas, too gently to combine
10. Distribute among the containers, store for 2 days

To Serve: Top with the avocado dressing and enjoy

Nutrition Facts Per Serving (without dressing): Calories:640 | Total Fat: 51g| Total Carbs: 9.8g| Protein: 38.8g

Conclusion

Now you've come to the end of my Mediterranean Diet Plan Cookbook. I hope you enjoy planning your week out in advance with my recipes, and sharing the meals – and maybe a little wine - with love ones and friends. Not only that, I hope that this cookbook becomes a useful tool that will help you stay healthy, happy and full!

28250654R00061

Printed in Great Britain
by Amazon